THE REFERENCE SHELF   VOLUME 36 NUMBER 5

THE DRIVE
AGAINST ILLITERACY

EDITED BY IRWIN ISENBERG

Associate Editor, Foreign Policy Association

THE H. W. WILSON COMPANY
NEW YORK   1964

THE REFERENCE SHELF

The books in this series reprint articles, excerpts from books, and addresses on current issues, social trends, and other aspects of American life, and occasional surveys of foreign countries. There are six separately bound numbers in each volume, all of which are generally published in the same calendar year. One number is a collection of recent speeches on a variety of subjects; each of the remaining numbers is devoted to a single subject and gives background information and discussion from varying points of view, followed by a comprehensive bibliography.

Subscribers to the current volume receive the books as issued. The subscription rate is $12 ($15 foreign) for a volume of six numbers. The price of single numbers is $3 each.

PREFACE

Illiteracy and poverty are linked in a tragic bond throughout the continents. At least 700 million people in the world today are illiterate. Almost all of them live in the underdeveloped two thirds of the globe. Burdened by poverty and shackled by illiteracy, they face the most tremendous obstacles in their struggle for even a minimum of economic improvement. The result is often frustration and unrest.

In recent years, as the articles in the first section of this book indicate, many underdeveloped nations have launched ambitious educational programs to cut down on the number of their adult illiterates. Many countries are also making determined efforts to improve and expand educational facilities for the young. But lack of money, a shortage of trained personnel, and population increases have all conspired to make the way to progress slow and difficult. Nevertheless, there is a global awareness that a basic part of the drive for economic development must consist of a frontal attack on illiteracy.

In the United States, outright illiteracy amounts to 2.4 per cent of the population, somewhat more than 3 million people, according to the 1960 census. However, there are more than 8 million so-called functional illiterates in the country. These are people who have completed less than five years of school and who, presumably, are unable to understand written instructions or perform adequately any of the reading or writing tasks that are a routine part of daily life. Additional millions of Americans have gone beyond the elementary grades, but they still lack sufficient reading skills.

Such deficiencies seriously handicap the individual in our society. Most of the illiterates and functional illiterates in the United States, for example, are on the lowest rungs of the economic ladder. It is becoming harder for them to find a place in our mechanized, automated economy. All too often they find the doors barred.

The signs of undereducation are frequently a place on the welfare rolls, a home in the slums, and, perhaps, worst of all, the absence of any real hope for the future. As the articles in the last three sections of this compilation show, there is considerable concern about undereducation in the United States. What are its causes? What are the links between the underprivileged and the undereducated? What can be done to overcome the problem?

A start has been made. Many communities in the country have set up special courses for the undereducated. The Federal Government has also designed programs to teach basic reading, writing, and comprehension skills to adults. The underprivileged, from whom stem the undereducated of the future, are also receiving considerable attention.

The problem is complex, the need immediate. Much remains to be done before the future can become more promising than it now is to the millions of undereducated Americans. It is a matter of helping these people help themselves so that their talents can be developed, their abilities utilized, their horizons broadened. This is a goal eminently suited to a democratic society.

The editor wishes to thank the authors and publishers who have generously granted permission to reprint the materials included in this book.

Irwin Isenberg

August 1964

CONTENTS

I. THE WORLD-WIDE STRUGGLE AGAINST ILLITERACY

EDITOR'S INTRODUCTION

For centuries a large percentage of the world's people lived and worked without being able to read or write. In many cases, for instance among those who were part of primitive or agricultural economies, the lack of literacy was not necessarily a serious drawback. The ability to make a living and even prosper did not always depend upon the ability to read and write.

The revolution in world politics since the end of World War II, however, has caused profound changes in the attitudes of men and nations. Almost every country is committed to some form of planned economic development. Part of the over-all plan usually concerns the raising of educational levels so that the nation may be better equipped, in terms of human resources, to deal with the technological, industrial, and scientific challenges thrust upon it by the twentieth century.

The articles in this section indicate the close relationship between the educational process and social and economic progress. The first article speaks of the deep-rooted barriers to literacy that exist in many parts of the world and suggests the need for creating the proper stimuli for education. This is followed by a discussion of the conditions which foster literacy as well as those, such as child labor, which impede the drive for the spread of basic education. A United Nations Educational, Scientific and Cultural Organization (UNESCO) report, which speaks of the current world-wide battle against illiteracy, emphasizes that the right to education is a basic human right.

The last two articles show what efforts are being made on the national and local level. They illustrate the eagerness with which people learn if given the opportunity. At the same time these articles stress, once again, the magnitude of the problem.

THE POOL OF IGNORANCE [1]

The world's vast pools of ignorance are located in Asia, particularly South and Southeast Asia, the Middle East, most of Africa, and Central and South America. Throughout most of these areas, as in India, Pakistan, Indonesia and Vietnam, above 80 per cent of the populations are unable to read or write, while in Afghanistan, Saudi-Arabia, French West Africa and Ethiopia, the percentage embraces from 95 to 99 per cent of the adults. Except for Argentina and Uruguay, the number of illiterates everywhere in Central and South America exceeds a fifth of each country's citizenry. In Bolivia, Peru, Brazil, Guatemala, and Haiti, for instance, less than half the people can read or write.

Just as illiteracy diminishes as one moves from the poverty-stricken to the more opulent countries, so too within most nations the degree of literacy rises with increases in national and personal income, with movement from rural to urban areas, and with escape from "minority" status. In the United States, for example, the incidence of illiteracy rises dramatically as investigators move from young, high-income, urban, white males to aged, low-income, rural, colored males. Small wonder then that the UN has premised its fundamental education programs on the assumption that literacy, while important to a community's economic progress, is basically an instrument designed to enhance human dignity and creativity—and as such is a universal human right.

Nevertheless, the seemingly manifest virtues of literacy are by no means accepted by everyone. Within many communities motivations favoring it may be lacking or may run the gamut of extremes. A century ago the great California rancheros lived idyllic lives, perfectly content with their incapacity to read or write. And during recent investigations in West Africa an American educator discovered that among nonliterate tribes of that area attitudes varied from "complete self-satisfaction" with their illiterate condition to a "burning desire" for literacy. In all times and places, of course, certain vested interests have profited by

[1] From article by C. K. Yearley, Jr., a member of the history department at the University of Florida. *Commonweal.* 71:175-7. N. 6, '59. Reprinted by permission.

ignorance. The master class of the Old South frowned on the extension of such basic skills to the slave community. Again, in primitive or underdeveloped areas visited by UN and other educational field teams—Haiti, Jamaica, and parts of Africa, for instance—literacy is opposed by medicine men, chieftains or political leaders, lawyers or merchants who prey on the ignorant.

Experts are agreed that until literacy becomes one of the conscious needs of the group or community it is almost pointless to try promoting it; consequently in many places the primary educational task is stimulating such consciousness. Examples of how such an awareness arises are fairly numerous. In one impoverished nonliterate community an education team invited a successful farmer from a nearby town to discuss local problems with them. While describing his own procedures in soil preparation, planting, and crop care, he cited the information furnished him by agricultural bulletins. Almost immediately farmers in the nonliterate group realized that their success was likely to be contingent on their ability to read, and requests for literacy training swelled.

But the stimuli to literacy vary widely. At times individuals will strive to attain literacy as the result of powerful inner drives for higher status. In other instances literacy becomes the group's way of coping with daily, often vexing, community problems— improving sanitary conditions or the water supply, checking diseases, caring for children, balancing diets, raising better livestock, reading signs to avoid danger or to locate streets. In still other cases it has been and still is an instrument of nationalism or a means of purveying or perpetuating an ideology.

In the United States justification for compulsory public education has often been tied to the argument that a democratic society will prove viable only as long as it rests on an informed and educated populace, and the corollary that our technology requires a sustained flow of skilled hands and trained minds. Similarly, the remarkable reductions of illiteracy in the Soviet Union—only one Russian in twenty-five is illiterate—have been closely coupled with the technical and ideological aspirations of the whole society—at least as the state sees them. Yet even where the desired incentives or popular motivations exist, obstacles are still so formidable that only the most massive assaults on illiteracy appear likely to produce results that will impress those who view the problem with a sense of urgency.

Sustained, dedicated, well-financed programs of mass education pursued by national governments are, undoubtedly, the most effective antidote to widespread ignorance. Unhappily, however, such attacks are completely beyond the capacity of many nations and territories. As a consequence, since the end of World War II, part of the burden of formulating and helping inaugurate such efforts in backward regions has been assumed by UNESCO. Collaborating with about fifty member states of the UN, it has pioneered fundamental education in many regions of the world through a series of pilot projects. Basically, however, it has functioned best as an international brain trust, bringing educational specialists together, sponsoring colloquia and seminars, helping recruit, train and advise field teams. By collecting information from numerous quarters it has served as a clearing house for ideas while simultaneously dramatizing the human dimensions of world ignorance.

Moreover, UNESCO has sponsored research and analysis of its own and made substantial contributions to the elaboration of new techniques. Thus in places where conditions are too primitive to begin educational processes with reading and writing —often because no written language even exists—it has guided the development of preliteracy campaigns. Elsewhere its specialists have encouraged the simplification of scripts and helped resolve problems posed by two languages, one classical or scholarly, the other more commonplace; they have devised new manuals for field workers, given advice on new texts, and stimulated adult education movements. Frequently work launched by UNESCO at the international level dovetails with the efforts of church groups or campaigns by local civic organizations.

Nothing suggests that people engaged in such work are deluded romantics; UNESCO and other specialists, in their own statements, recognize the feebleness of their influence on world illiteracy. Men's values are still such that UNESCO's budget is less than the cost of a dozen large jet bombers. Nations that might conceivably divert more badly needed funds to education often spend exorbitant amounts on armaments; governments frequently invest scarce talents and resources in dramatic political programs, or vote-catching experiments designed to capitalize on nationalist or anti-imperialist sentiment.

Frequently, too, basic problems are even more varied and serious than this. In some societies the desire for literacy simply does not exist; in others, such as the Marbial Valley of Haiti, where there is often a commendable urge to learn, the obstacles are almost overwhelming. Where schools function they are poverty stricken, teachers are badly undertrained, texts are obsolescent and confusing, conflicts between languages prove baffling; endemic disease and the demands of local agriculture eat into attendance. Elsewhere schooling can be continued for only three or four years—not enough to insure permanent literacy: barring substantial adult literacy campaigns children are commonly reabsorbed by the nonliterate community. Nowhere is it possible for schools to rise above the society that creates them.

Studies of previous advances in the fight for literacy clearly indicate that illiteracy can be cut by as much as 30 to 40 per cent in a decade—under favorable conditions. But, again, the rates of progress demonstrated over the past in places where the incidence of illiteracy was highest leave no doubt whatever that unless prodigious efforts are undertaken to curtail it, improvement will prove negligible. The latest figures for prepartition India, for example, show a decennial rate of progress of 1 per cent. In other words, at this rate it would take India a century to increase the number of literates by 10 per cent; similarly, the last reported progress in Egypt would produce a mere 15 per cent increase in literacy over the next fifty years. Admittedly these figures may now be hopelessly inaccurate, since in the case of India, Egypt and many other countries, the last such calculations were made twenty to thirty years ago; nonetheless, they bare something of the magnitude of the task, and permit no unduly sanguine views of what lies ahead.

To be sure, illiteracy is not invariably a major tragedy. There are cultures, however primitive, so well adjusted to their environment and so isolated from the more modern aspirations of the race that the absence of such skills is not missed. In Laos, Cambodia and parts of Indonesia, for instance, there are peoples whose agriculture keeps them in a comfortable competence and upon whom literacy, given their present interests, would confer few immediate benefits. Similarly, literacy can scarcely be regarded as a matter of great urgency in secluded places such as Tibet, where religion and otherworldly predilections dominate.

Likewise, if illiteracy is not necessarily tragic, literacy when and where it exists is assuredly not a panacea for men's ills. At best it is one instrument of opportunity, useful only to the extent that other forms of social progress accompany it. The real tragedy of such ignorance, it may be, becomes manifest only among men who are infatuated by glimpses of higher standards of living, whom modern science and technology, nationalism or anti-imperialism have induced to strike for modernization and industrialism, whose attitudes toward their environments are no longer resigned, and whose hopes have far outrun their capacities.

Hundreds of millions of these men and women, moreover, are no longer beyond the mainstream of world events. Their frustrations—and aspirations—bear intimately upon the character of world politics, upon the world's increasingly interdependent economy, upon the freedom of individual and international intercourse. They bear, too, upon the climate of reason that will prevail among future generations and, not least, upon whatever peace these generations will know.

OBSTACLES TO PROGRESS [2]

Through the years, the enlightened nations have fostered literacy in the belief that life in a democracy where all citizens

[2] From "World Literacy and Education," by Gertrude Hildreth, professor of education, Brooklyn College. *School and Society.* 89:371-2. N. 4, '61. Reprinted by permission.

participate on a basis of equality requires a common foundation of knowledge. Through reading people learn about human rights, and everyone has at hand a means of self-improvement, self-fulfillment, and enlightened, independent action. In December 1960, a resolution presented to a general conference of UNESCO in Paris stated, "Education and training hold the key not only to the material welfare of the newly independent countries but also to the very stability of the new states."

Although adults in backward countries can learn to read and write readily enough . . . instruction in literacy during the childhood years has definite advantages. Young children are less inhibited than adults in response to every new experience and less sensitive to status. Furthermore, boys and girls are more nearly on an equal footing socially. In some parts of the world there is more opposition to adult literacy programs than to the extension of primary schooling. Adult literacy campaigns tend to lapse after initial enthusiasm dies down, whereas primary schooling is more apt to become a permanent feature of social progress in a new nation. The reluctance of women in backward countries to appear in public presents a serious obstacle to women's education.

Fortunately, literacy rates around the world have been steadily rising as educational opportunities for the common people become more widespread. As the new nations reach independent status, their governments are making long-range plans for liquidating illiteracy through educational programs both for children and adults. . . .

No nation ever has banished illiteracy without a state-supported, free school system for children of all classes, with attendance obligatory for children from the age of six or seven to eleven or twelve. Fifty years ago, Russia was among the backward nations in high rate of illiteracy. Today, in the Soviet Union, less than 10 per cent of the population is illiterate, according to recent estimates, an improvement that is the direct result of establishing universal primary schooling.

The rise of literacy in modern Turkey illustrates the progress that has come about through vast social and economic changes and the establishment of a secular state-supported school system. Literacy has risen from less than 10 per cent when the republic was founded in 1923 to nearly 60 per cent at the present time. Formerly, boys made up over 80 per cent of the primary school enrollment and girls less than 20 per cent. Today, these percentages are practically equal.

Illiteracy scarcely gained a foothold in the United States, even though our country had to contend with waves of immigration from countries where illiteracy was high. The foreign elements were gradually assimilated; the children learned to speak English and were caught up in the net of common public schools. The enactment and enforcement of school attendance laws increased the percentage of the school-age population attending in each generation, particularly from 1900 onward. Then came mechanization of industry and transportation which eliminated the need for child labor and made schooling available even in remote areas. Mechanical printing and typesetting produced more textbooks and a flood of literature suited to all ages, tastes, and levels of readability.

In planning programs of assistance for underdeveloped nations, the question arises as to the relative importance of technical assistance and aid to education. A British authority, H. L. Elvin, has pointed out the dilemma this problem creates for the underdeveloped countries. These countries, he says, cannot develop a modern economy, modern administration, and modern society without better and much more widespread education; and they cannot develop an adequate system of education without a more modernized economy, administration and society. A century ago, Count Leo Tolstoy questioned the value of roads, the telegraph, new literature, and other amenities for a backward Russia in which, as he estimated, only one per cent of 70 million people were literate.

Literacy in our country progressed hand in hand with technology; conditions of life improved as the mass of the people became better educated. In Israel, in Japan, and in the Soviet Union, economic development and social development have advanced together. . . .

Diversity of tongues is one of the greatest stumbling blocks in the way of establishing common school education and teaching literacy. In India, there are fifteen major languages, plus several hundred dialects. In Africa, there are over eight hundred different languages and dialects, most of them spoken by small groups or tribes. To establish universal literacy, the Soviet Union has had to provide instructional materials and programs in over fifty languages in addition to standard Russian.

Another obstacle arises from the fact that provisions for elementary education, like health services, scarcely can keep pace with the rapidly expanding population in backward countries. In Latin America, this is the greatest threat to the present economy and to social progress.

The obstacles to education are greater in agricultural regions where the population is sparse, child labor is traditional, and the prejudices and indifference of the people are difficult to overcome. An economy that depends on children's employment at menial tasks—field work, housework, handicrafts, and early apprenticeships—must be changed if elementary schooling is to become established. Exploitation of children as wage earners by parents and employers perpetuates the blight of ignorance and illiteracy. Every child, regardless of economic status or social class, should receive at least the rudiments of common school education before being employed as a worker.

In some parts of the world, the establishment of national systems of secular schools still meets with resistance. In others, there is no free schooling supported by general taxation, and poverty-stricken families are unable to pay even the smallest fees for tuition.

The task of educating the world's children is gigantic, but it can be accomplished through the tremendous resources now at our command. As a basis for scientific planning for educational provisions in backward countries, new data should be obtained that indicate the proportion of children of school age who attend and who fail to attend primary school for several consecutive years.

Literacy programs will require more teachers, particularly experts in all phases of language instruction, than in any previous period of history. Our country can help by sending to the new nations and less-developed countries an educational task force to train native leaders and teachers. In turn, a larger number of foreign teachers could be trained here for educational work in the homeland.

THE DEVELOPMENT DECADE [3]

The United Nations Development Decade has just begun. During this decade the United Nations and its specialized agencies are pledged to mobilize their past experiences and coordinate their present efforts in a sustained attack upon disease, hunger, ignorance and poverty. The member governments of the United Nations have set their seal of approval on this program, and each of the United Nations agencies has pledged its support.

The struggle against ignorance and illiteracy itself will demand a major concentration of effort. Examination of available statistics discloses that an average of almost 50 per cent—in some regions 70-80 per cent or more—of the adult population is illiterate; in numerical terms this represents something more than 700 million people. The rapidly increasing world population, together with the inevitable time lag required to bring to complete fruition plans for the provision of universal primary education, makes it certain that these numbers will increase, rather than decrease, during the Development Decade unless adult illiteracy is most energetically tackled now. The world population was estimated at . . . [1.55 billion] in 1900, and at the present rate of increase may be . . . [6 billion] by the year 2000. Thus, even where percentages of illiteracy fall, the actual numbers of illiterates are growing in several countries. It is urgently necessary to arrest this growth.

[3] From *World Campaign for Universal Literacy*, report issued by the United Nations Educational, Scientific and Cultural Organization (UNESCO). Paris. My. 15, '63. p 36-9, 82. Reprinted by permission.

Already in Africa, Asia and Latin America great programs for the development of formal education are being undertaken. Devoting as much as 4 per cent of their gross national product to the task, some seventy countries plan to complete the provision of universal primary education by 1980 or before. These plans undoubtedly constitute the greatest single weapon in the battle against illiteracy.

Nevertheless unless an attack is made on the problem of widespread adult illiteracy simultaneously with the effort to provide universal primary education, many of the hopes for the future may fail and success will most certainly be delayed. It cannot be emphasized too strongly that the enormous reservoir of adult illiteracy presents the greatest threat to the success of the Development Decade and to hopes and plans for raising standards of living throughout the world.

The illiterate person is a weak link in the whole chain of development. He is the person who is "outside public affairs." This is not only a personal tragedy for the individuals concerned, who are not just ciphers, but men and women whose dignity and human rights must be respected; it is also, for the nations affected, an economic straitjacket which must be shed if true progress is to be made.

The success of primary schooling is dangerously undermined in areas where there is widespread adult illiteracy. Many children are discouraged from enrolling at school, and large numbers are permitted to leave before they have completed the course and before they have become fully literate. Even when it is possible to make attendance compulsory, many who return to live in illiterate communities soon lose the knowledge they had acquired at school and relapse into illiteracy. The fact that a majority of the illiterates are women has deplorable consequences on home life and the education of children. Indeed, through no fault of their own, illiterate men and women constitute a drag on the development of their country and are in turn deprived of their rightful share in its progress.

For these reasons, it is considered that during the Development Decade it will be essential to attack the problems of primary schooling and adult illiteracy simultaneously.

In mobilizing for the fight against illiteracy and maintaining the battle until it is won, certain measures need to be taken. Aims and objectives must be defined; the necessary administrative and supporting organization must be established; facilities for the training of the full-time and part-time volunteer teachers must be developed. The large volume of materials required must be prepared and produced. Some of the newer media now being exploited, such as radio, television, and other devices, may prove of great assistance, and many countries are already investigating their possibilities.

Moreover, in the changing pattern of education in the twentieth century, the development of continuing opportunities for adult education is seen by educationists the world over as a necessity of our time. Literacy by itself is but the door for entry into all those opportunities of a wider context of adult education which countries, unimpeded by the set patterns inherited from the past, are now free to develop. This in itself is perhaps the most exciting educational challenge and opportunity of our times.

The resources, both in manpower and means, needed to launch and maintain bold programs for the eradication of illiteracy, are not small. But the battle against world illiteracy is only a part, albeit an urgent and essential part, of the plans for a great stride forward in the Development Decade. The means and resources to combat illiteracy will not be exhausted and obsolete when the battle is won; they do not involve a special "emergency" expenditure relevant only to eradicating illiteracy. They represent an investment in permanent and basic tools, in trained manpower and physical means, which will be essential in any case if the tempo of future development is to be increased and the possibilities enlarged.

The primary responsibility for effective, energetic action against illiteracy must remain with the member states themselves since this action depends for its success on mobilizing the hearts and minds and the will of all the people. Without this mobilization, backed by the national, political and administrative acceptance of its importance, no hopeful aspiration or outside aid will achieve the necessary results. . . .

Definitions and Objectives

Literacy is not simply the ability to sign one's name or to read or write a few simple sentences. Even the simplest description, such as that which defines literacy for census purposes, should not be less than that proposed by an Expert Committee on the Standardization of Educational Statistics convened in 1951 by UNESCO, namely:

A person is literate who can with understanding both read and write a short, simple statement on his everyday life.

The Meeting of Experts on Literacy which was convened by UNESCO in June 1962 was unanimous that the aim must be for functional literacy and considered that:

A person is literate when he has acquired the essential knowledge and skills which enable him to engage in all those activities in which literacy is required for effective functioning in his group and community, and whose attainments in reading, writing and arithmetic make it possible for him to continue to use these skills towards his own and the community's development and for active participation in the life of his country.

In quantitative terms, the standard of attainment in functional literacy may be equated to the skills of reading, writing and arithmetic achieved after a set number of years of primary or elementary schooling.

Mass illiteracy should not be regarded as an isolated problem requiring only temporary special measures, even though a massive attack on it is now urgently required. The fact that so large a part of the world's population is at present illiterate clearly indicates the need for special emphasis in this particular area of adult education. But education for literacy is only a necessary preliminary stage to the wide opportunities for adult education which must be provided if the literacy program is to be meaningful.

Hence, the attainment of literacy is a most important means for, and has the objective of, enabling a person to develop his full potential and to participate more fully and constructively in the life of the community. It should be the first step to a continuing program of adult education which should be considered part of the total educational provision. . . .

The Right to Education is a basic human right which must be made a reality for all men within the Development Decade. It is in men's minds that human progress is conceived and planned; it is by their wisdom, knowledge and skill that it must be achieved. If literacy then is the foundation of effective and continuing education, education, in its turn, is the very infrastructure of development.

Education is thus seen as a prerequisite of material progress; but it is no less a preparation for its proper use and enjoyment. The Development Decade will fail in its real test if it succeeds only in raising the gross national product of each member state, in increasing output, expanding mechanization and industrialization, achieving higher levels of prosperity and more leisure. These attainments will indeed make a very limited contribution to human happiness unless they are accompanied by moral, cultural and artistic achievements; nor will they disperse the clouds of mistrust and fear and the menace of war which cast their shadows on mankind, unless they help to bring about a wider appreciation of the common aspirations of the human race, an attachment to the ideals of peace, mutual respect and deeper understanding among peoples. To the struggle for these intangible but vital objectives of the Development Decade education must lend its full support.

START OF A GREAT BATTLE [4]

During a trip to Ecuador two years ago, I visited a little village on the shores of Lake Otvalo. It was a Sunday but I noticed a party of Indians working with unaccustomed vigor, carrying

[4] From "70 Million Illiterates," by Oscar Vera, professor of sociology and education at the Pedagogical Institute of the University of Chile and coordinator of UNESCO's project for the extension of primary education in Latin America. Reprinted from *The UNESCO Courier*. 14:33-5. Je. '61.

stones, leveling the ground and digging out the foundations for what was to be a school.

Three or four months later when I revisited the village, I found that the little school was finished—built by voluntary labor and with some help from the authorities, who paid for materials the village was too poor to buy. Eighty very well-behaved small boys were seated on the simple school benches doing their lessons under the supervision of a woman teacher.

Today, the same thing is happening over and over again in village communities of Mexico, Bolivia, Peru, Guatemala and nearly all the Latin American countries—a striking testimony to the efforts that men and women are willing to make so that the new generation may enjoy a fuller life. Such endeavors encourage the governments of all countries in the region to build schools and extend education, and thus remove one of the gravest obstacles to social and economic development—illiteracy.

The proportion of illiterates in Latin America (approximately 40 per cent of the population above the age of fifteen) is still high in comparison with the United States, Japan, or the majority of European countries, though it has been considerably reduced from the beginning-of-the-century figure of over 80 per cent. We must remember, however, that despite the common origin and closely related cultural traditions of the twenty Latin American countries, conditions vary considerably not only from one country to another, but even within the individual countries.

In several of them (Mexico, Guatemala, Ecuador, Peru, Bolivia) large groups of the original Indian inhabitants have lived through conquest, colonial periods and the years of independence without ever becoming completely assimilated in the national life. They still preserve many of their native characteristics.

In all Latin American countries agriculture predominates, and in almost all of them most people live in the country. Consequently there is a profound disparity in living conditions between the considerable urban development, comparable in many respects to that of the more advanced countries, and the extremely backward state of the rural masses. These differences are evident from economic, social and cultural standpoints. . . .

Generally speaking it is the poorest countries, with a predominantly rural population, which have had the most difficulty in expanding their education services. There are, however, certain exceptions, which are worth mentioning because they suggest that the backwardness or progress of a country's educational system is determined not merely by high or low income, but by other factors as well.

Costa Rica, for example, is a small agricultural country which boasts that its schoolteachers constitute its only army. The proportion of illiterates is as low there as in the most advanced countries of the continent. On the other hand, Venezuela, with the highest per capita income in Latin America (thanks to its huge oil reserves) has a comparatively high percentage of illiteracy. Since 1958, however, the Venezuelan Government has been making a vigorous effort and in the near future, through the judicious use of its resources, will bring education to the whole school-age population. In this way, within the next few years, illiteracy will have been uprooted at its source.

The percentage of illiteracy cannot alone give an idea of how far education has been developed, or to what extent it reaches the population as a whole. Thus, for instance, the proportion of illiterates in the United States and Japan is less than 3 per cent; yet the average educational level of the population in the two countries is respectively 9 and 7.2 years of schooling. In other words, in the United States the average adult has attended school for nine years, and in Japan for only seven.

From this standpoint the average educational level of the Latin American population in 1950 was two years—ranging from six months' school attendance in the country with the least developed educational system to just over four years in the most educationally advanced. It takes about four years of school attendance to attain what specialists call "functional literacy." . . .

As a distinguished Brazilian educator has put it, education in Latin America is the privilege of a small minority which has access to the various levels of the educational system, while the great majority of the population is neither equipped to make an effective contribution to economic development nor able to take a full share in democratic life.

The two main reasons for this situation are school absenteeism and school-leaving. Many children do not go to school either because their parents, even when they recognize the value of education, cannot do without the extra income from the children's work, or simply because there is no local school for them to attend.

A very high proportion of those who do start school never complete the full course. Less than 25 per cent of the children who enroll in primary schools stay on to the end of the compulsory education period.

In 1959 primary school enrollments in Latin America stood at about 25 million, out of a total of 37 million children of school age. About a third of the children were therefore not attending school. To provide proper education for them at the right time would mean building about 400,000 classrooms, training an equal number of teachers, and recruiting the corresponding administrative staff and inspectors.

There is also the problem of providing equipment and teaching materials. Finally, some financial assistance must be given to poor children or to their families.

Such measures, and others of a purely pedagogic nature, would get rid of absenteeism. They would also considerably reduce school-leaving, which reaches alarming proportions in nearly all the countries concerned, especially in rural districts. They would also eradicate illiteracy within a few years.

The Latin American countries have decided to undertake this formidable task. But it is a particularly difficult one for them not only because of their underdeveloped economies but also because of the tremendous speed at which their populations are increasing. While the total world population is growing at the rate of 1.6 per cent per annum, the annual rate of increase in Latin America is 2.6 per cent, and in a number of countries it exceeds 3 per cent.

This calls for a far greater effort to maintain adequate educational services than is required in other countries. It is not only necessary because of the rapid and tremendous growth of the population, but also because the proportion of those over twenty years of age who can make an effective contribution to economic life in all its aspects, and pay for the education of their juniors, is less than 50 per cent in nearly all the Latin American countries. In other countries, where population increase is more gradual, the proportion is from 65 to 70 per cent.

Without neglecting adult education campaigns, the only means of rapidly bringing illiterate adults into full participation in community life and fitting them for new economic activities, the Latin American countries are concentrating their efforts on extirpating illiteracy at its root. One of the most important weapons in this campaign is making primary education available to the whole school-age population. These countries have therefore been playing an active part, since 1956, in an unprecedented venture, UNESCO's Major Project for the Extension of Primary Education in Latin America.

Despite the short time this project has been in operation, encouraging results have already been obtained. Between 1956 and 1959, primary school attendance in Latin America increased by about 4 million, while the number of teachers rose by more than 90,000. In certain countries the increase in primary school enrollments was positively sensational: 40 per cent in Honduras in the past three years; 40 per cent in Venezuela since 1958; 40 per cent in a single year in Cuba, where the government has decided to make 1961 "education year" and plans to eliminate illiteracy completely by providing schools for the whole of the school-age population and conducting a vigorous adult education campaign.

Brazil and Mexico, which between them account for half the population of Latin America, have increased their primary school attendance by 22 per cent and 18 per cent respectively in the past three years. All countries, in varying degrees, are adopting measures which testify to an increasingly firm determination to extend and improve their educational services. They have resolved that in ten years' time there shall be schools available for all their children.

THE MAGIC OF WORDS [5]

Maria Pequena de Souza's eyes filled with tears when she saw what she had written on the paper before her.

Scrawled across the sheet, heedless of the orderly blue lines, was the word *belota* (tassel). Mrs. de Souza, thirty-two years old and the mother of six children, cried with emotion. It was the first word she had written in her life.

Little more than a month later, Mrs. de Souza wrote a letter to President João Goulart [ousted from office in April 1964]. The spelling was bad, and the grammar was colloquial, but her words conveyed a clear picture of the anguish of the poor in Brazil's backward northeast region.

"I beg you, sir, for scholarships for my children, because I can't educate them. I work day and night washing by day and ironing at night, so they shall not want. Their father, with six children at home, gets 300 cruzeiros (50 cents) for a day's service. How are we to get by?" Mrs. de Souza wrote.

Literacy in 40 Hours

Mrs. de Souza learned to read and write in only forty hours of group instruction through an adult literacy project, supported by the Alliance for Progress, in this state of Rio Grande do Norte.

The Brazilian northeast, a nine-state region containing 23 million people, probably has 8 million adult illiterates such as Mrs. de Souza was before she took the course. The Alliance for Progress target is to wipe out this illiteracy by 1970.

No other program in the United States-aided effort to improve economic and social conditions in the northeast has the potential for political reform of the literacy campaign.

[5] From "Brazil Conducts a Literacy Drive," by Juan de Onis, New York *Times* correspondent. New York *Times*. p 18. Je. 2, '63. © 1963 by The New York Times Company. Reprinted by permission.

"We are not just trying to teach people to read and write. We intend through the literacy program to make these people capable of being citizens," said Philip Schwab, education coordinator of the United States Agency for International Development in Recife, the Alliance for Progress headquarters for the northeast.

Political Message Injected

The literacy course contains a civic, even political message. As they learn to read, the adults are told that "the vote is the arm of the people," "education is for both the rich and the poor" and "agrarian reform is an urgent need."...

Rio Grande do Norte, which is leading in the literacy campaign, is a relatively little state with a population of just over a million people. The state's plan is to teach 100,000 adults to read and write by the end of Governor Aluisio Alves's term in 1966.

Idea of University Group

The literacy campaign got started here through the efforts of a group of university students and young professors. They obtained the support of Francisco Calazans Fernandez, the State Secretary of Education, and the program was included in the $3 million United States aid grant for education in Rio Grande do Norte.

The first project was started in Angicos, a typical municipality of the interior, where 75 per cent of the 9,540 inhabitants work in the cotton fields or on salt flats. The course began with 380 adult illiterates. "When the first rains came in February, we lost half the men, who left to work in the fields, but some sent their children to complete the course," said Carlo Lira, a professor of philosophy, who was a course coordinator.

After thirty-six hours of literacy and civic-orientation classes, 150 adults completed the course, and 135 were considered literate on the basis of written tests and letters written to President Goulart. The students were also graded on political awareness....

The audio-visual method for the course was devised by Professor Paulo Freire of the University of Recife. Commonly used words are chosen that can be pictured on a slide. The first word that Senhora de Souza wrote, *belota*, means a tassel that adorns the riding crops used by local horsemen.

Once the word has been fixed graphically for the students by slides, it is broken into its phonetic parts, and the students build words phonetically. Then they go on to write words.

II. THE UNDEREDUCATED MILLIONS

EDITOR'S INTRODUCTION

Functional illiteracy (sometimes called undereducation) is a coldly clinical phrase used to describe the state of those Americans whose literacy skills are so limited as to make it increasingly difficult for them to find and hold jobs. While the functionally illiterate are considered to be those with less than five years of education, an estimated 23 million adult Americans lack an eighth-grade education. In terms of the demands of our economy, a majority of these people probably should be considered undereducated. This is more than a statistic. It is a statement of individual hardship and tragedy, of limited horizons and wasted talents, of despair and social dynamite.

The articles in this section are devoted to an examination of the lives of the educationally handicapped Americans. The first two articles comment on the extent of illiteracy and near illiteracy in the United States. They make it clear that it may be many more decades before the problem is resolved. The second article also pinpoints the groups, areas, and occupations where functional illiteracy is most prevalent.

Bernard Asbell's article from *McCall's* then shows, with painful clarity, the shattering impact of undereducation on the individual. One conclusion to be drawn is that the vast majority of these people have a bleak future. A lost generation is what Michael Harrington in his New York *Times Magazine* article calls today's undereducated and often unemployable youth. But there is also glimmer of hope. For though the opportunities for improvement offered to the undereducated are far from adequate, there have been increased efforts in our national mobilization to meet the educational problems of our less fortunate citizens.

The next articles in this section deal with other aspects of undereducation. Robert Luke speaks of the unproductiveness of the undereducated. Eli Ginzberg asks whether a democratic society can function effectively when so many of its citizens are on the borderline of illiteracy. Edward Warner Brice discusses the plight of the functionally illiterate in our industrialized society and describes literacy training programs undertaken by governmental and private agencies.

"Truly," as President Johnson has said, "a monumental task lies ahead. . . . I urge prompt action on proposed programs for combatting adult illiteracy, for expanding adult education, for improving the quality of education at all levels."

THE UNDEREDUCATED [1]

As a result of compulsory public education, illiteracy has been on the decline in the United States for many years. There is every reason to believe that it will continue to decline in the years ahead. But the rate of decline is slow; analyses of census data indicate that there will be millions of illiterates of working age in the population for decades. And modern urban society has fewer and fewer places for persons with so severe an educational handicap.

In earlier times, a responsible adult with little or no competency in reading or writing had relatively little difficulty finding employment and maintaining a stable family life. An illiterate might even possess certain skills not requiring a command of the written language which would gain for him a satisfactory income and the respect of the community. The situation today is very different. There are progressively fewer jobs which an illiterate is able to fill.

The direct connection between illiteracy and unemployment became sharply apparent when government programs were started to retrain workers displaced by automation, other technological change, or the migration of industry. Secretary of Labor Wirtz told a House Education subcommittee . . . that early experience

[1] From "Illiteracy in the United States," by Helen B. Shaffer, staff writer, *Editorial Research Reports*. *Editorial Research Reports*. 1, no 17:329-37. My. 1, '63. Reprinted by permission.

under the Manpower Development and Training Act [see "Federal Aid for the Illiterate," Section IV, below] had illuminated the need for an additional program for adult basic education. "In attempting to get training programs under way," he said, "we have encountered repeatedly the depressing fact that many of our unemployed have such a low level of education that they cannot absorb the occupational training for the job openings we find." As a result, the very workers most in need of the opportunities which the act was designed to afford were unable in many cases to take advantage of them.

Recent data [Wirtz testified] indicate that more than 300,000 people looking for jobs had less than a fifth-grade education and almost one half million of those unemployed had less than an eighth-grade education. People so ill-prepared are at a competitive disadvantage in today's highly skilled labor market and will become progressively more disadvantaged as the nation pushes its way toward greater technological achievement.

Wirtz said that many of the hard-core unemployed were so deficient in reading and writing skills that they could not fill out applications for training or for jobs. One local employment office found it necessary to interview five hundred women before it could find thirty who were educationally qualified to enter a class in practical nurse training. So many applicants for a new training course for semiskilled maintenance and service jobs were unable to read labels on cans of cleaning materials and insecticides that the course was redesigned to devote half of each six-hour training period to basic education. The first report on the Manpower Development and Training Program, transmitted to Congress February 28 [1963], pointed out that the worker who could not read, write or use numbers with facility was handicapped not only because "his traditional job opportunities have diminished" but also because "he lacks the basic tools needed to upgrade his skills."

Illiteracy as Source of Dependency and Crime

To an increasing extent, a connection has been established between illiteracy and dependency, delinquency, illegitimacy, even disease. Assistant Secretary of Health, Education and Welfare Wilbur J. Cohen said at a joint hearing of two subcommittees of the House Committee on Education and Labor . . . [in 1962] that "we find the greatest incidence of poverty, disease, preventable accidents and personal maladjustment in occupational, home and civic life among the least educated." A large percentage of the 7.25 million persons receiving welfare payments —costing the taxpayer a total of $4.5 billion—are undereducated. Cohen also said that "45 per cent of all families with less than $2,000 of annual income, . . . families [which] . . . constitute the source from which the public welfare rolls develop," were headed by individuals with less than an eighth-grade education.

Low educational attainment [Cohen testified] is a prominent characteristic of mothers receiving welfare payments under the A.D.C. [Aid to Dependent Children] program. In New York . . . a 1957 study found almost a fifth of A.D.C. mothers had not gone beyond the fifth grade; in Louisiana, in 1954, half the A.D.C. mothers and three fourths of the fathers in the home had received a fifth-grade education or less. Illinois reported in 1960 that a fifth of their A.D.C. mothers never went beyond the sixth grade.

State and local welfare officials testified that illiterates and near-illiterates make up a large percentage of the nation's misfits. "They find it difficult to protect themselves . . . from irresponsible or malicious propaganda," one witness said. "People who are illiterate . . . present a source of danger to the community," another pointed out. "They are easily influenced by foreign philosophies." The illiterates were said to be gullible, easy prey for swindlers. . . .

The dictionary defines illiteracy as "inability to read and write." In a practical sense a person suffers the handicap of illiteracy if his ability to read and write is so limited that he cannot make ready use of these functions for ordinary purposes— if he cannot, for example, read labels, fill out forms, or write down messages. The Army during World War II used the term "functional illiteracy" to describe persons who were not absolutely illiterate but whose literacy level was so low that they could not understand written instructions about basic military tasks. Since then, the term "functional illiterate" has been used imprecisely to indicate various degrees of borderline literacy; the term is frequently applied to those who have completed fewer than five years of schooling.

The point of educational attainment short of which a person must as a rule be considered illiterate has never been satisfactorily determined. The United Nations Population Commission, in an effort to improve comparability of national census reports, recommended as a standard definition of literacy the "ability both to read and to write a simple message in any language." An Expert Committee on Standardization of Educational Statistics, appointed by the United Nations Educational, Scientific and Cultural Organization (UNESCO), suggested two classifications: "Semiliterate" to characterize a person who can read with understanding but cannot write a simple statement about something in his everyday life, and "illiterate" to describe a person who cannot read or write. A UN report on illiteracy several years ago warned against taking national enumerations of illiterates at face value, because the methods used to determine illiteracy tended to be "highly subjective and subject to error."

Steady Long-Term Decline of Illiteracy Rates

From 1840 through 1930, the United States Census Bureau gathered statistics on illiteracy by asking individuals whether they could read and write a simple message in any language. Beginning in 1940, that question was dropped and persons were asked to state instead how many years of schooling they had had. While years of schooling do not furnish an exact indication of an individual's level of literacy, such information is useful as a basis for estimating the extent of illiteracy and functional illiteracy.

Periodic special surveys by the Census Bureau have indicated the proportion of illiterates in population segments grouped by years of schooling. It was found in 1960, for example, that three fourths of those who never went to school were unable to read or write in any language. This absolute deficiency was characteristic also of 59 per cent of the individuals who had only one year of schooling, of 33 per cent of those with two years of schooling, of 17 per cent of persons who had been to school for three years, of 5 per cent of those who had gone for four years, and of 2 per cent of those with five years of schooling.

Analyses of 1960 census data indicated that there were 3,055,-000 illiterates in the fifty states that year; they represented 2.4 per cent of the population aged fourteen or more. The rate of absolute illiteracy has been going down steadily for nearly a century. The census of 1870 showed 5.7 million illiterates, or 20 per cent of the population ten years or more old.

Illiteracy rates vary regionally in much the same pattern today as in past decades. The highest rates are in the South, the lowest in parts of the West North Central, Mountain and Pacific areas. State rates of illiteracy in 1960 ranged from 6.3 per cent of persons aged fourteen or more in Louisiana down to 0.7 per cent in Iowa. States which had rates of 4 per cent or more included Alabama, Georgia, Hawaii, Louisiana, Mississippi, New Mexico, North Carolina, South Carolina and Texas. States with less than one per cent of illiteracy included Kansas, Idaho, Iowa, Nebraska, Oregon, South Dakota, Utah, Washington and Wyoming. All states had lower illiteracy rates in 1960 than in 1950. The drop was especially marked in high-rate states. The Louisiana rate, for example, had dropped 3½ percentage points; in other southern states, rates were down by two or more percentage points.

Illiteracy Among Negroes and the Foreign-Born

The high illiteracy rate in 1870 was due in large part to lack of education among the newly freed slaves. Four fifths of the Negroes were then illiterate, and they constituted nearly one half of all illiterates in the country at the time. . . . The 1930 census showed an illiteracy rate of 17.5 per cent among Negroes; the latest official estimate, for 1959, was 7.5 per cent.

The foreign-born no longer figure significantly, as they once did, in American illiteracy counts. Many immigrants who came to this country around the turn of the century were natives of sections of Europe where schooling was not available to the poorer classes. Entering low-grade employment or becoming wives of other immigrants shortly after arriving in the New World, many immigrants of that era "never got around" to learning to read and write. Immigration legislation of the early 1920's checked the intake of foreign-born illiterates and this class is now dying out. Illiteracy among native-born whites amounted to 6.2 per cent in 1890, but figures for the entire white population showed an illiteracy rate in 1959 of only 1.6 per cent.

New pockets of illiteracy have developed, however, among Spanish-speaking groups. The 1960 census showed that one million Puerto Ricans were then living in the continental United States. Of 269,000 Puerto Ricans aged twenty-five or more residing in New York City, 29 per cent had completed fewer than five years of schooling; similar percentages were indicated for Puerto Ricans in Jersey City and Philadelphia. Approximately 45 per cent of Spanish-speaking residents of the five southwestern states had less than five years of schooling. The illiteracy rate is particularly high among migrant agricultural workers.

Present Interest in the Functionally Illiterate

Official concern today centers primarily on the functionally illiterate—the undereducated whose ability to read, write and do simple arithmetic is at or below par for a fourth grader. This group includes not only those who have never finished the fifth grade but also many who went to school for as long as eight years but attended so sporadically or with so little interest that they never acquired a firm grasp on the basic skills for learning.

Estimates of the extent of functional illiteracy have to be based mostly on census reports of school attendance and thus tend to understate the proportions of the problem. Analysis of 1960 census data by the Department of Health, Education and Welfare showed that a total of more than 8.3 million persons aged twenty-five or more, or more than 8 per cent of the population in this age category, had completed less than five years of schooling and hence were to be considered "functional illiterates" in that they "lack, by and large, the background for effective performance as employees and citizens." In testimony in support of legislation for adult basic education, HEW officials discussed the problem in terms of some 11.4 million adults aged eighteen or more who had completed less than six years of schooling.

As a result of migrations of the poorly educated, some states ranking high in educational facilities and over-all educational attainment have large concentrations of illiterates in their big cities. New York State, where the percentage of the population with less than six years of schooling in 1960 was below the national average of 8.3 per cent, nevertheless had nearly 800,000 residents with less than five years of schooling—twice as many as North Carolina, where 17 per cent of the population had had less than six years of schooling. . . . Although low educational attainment is more prevalent among Negroes, it is by no means a nonwhite monopoly. A 1962 census survey showed that nearly 6 million whites and more than 2 million nonwhites in the fifty states had had less than five years of schooling or had had no schooling at all.

Illiteracy, even functional illiteracy, is sometimes referred to as a residual problem in the United States, because it results largely from inadequate educational facilities or insufficient enforcement of compulsory school attendance laws in the past. Inability to read and write with ease is most prevalent among older adults and so might be expected to disappear in time. Sterling M. McMurrin, then United States Commissioner of Education, told the House Education subcommittees . . . [in 1962] that "today, except for very special populations, such as migratory families, virtually all children who do not suffer from a pronounced physical or mental handicap attend schools," and therefore "one of the major causes of illiteracy in the past has been substantially eradicated."

Nevertheless, there appears to be too large a number of residual cases of illiteracy, and the rate at which illiteracy is disappearing seems too slow. McMurrin noted that in forty-one states for which there were data, the number of adults aged twenty-five or more who had completed less than five years of school had declined at a rate of only 100,000 a year between 1950 and 1960. He added that at that rate "it would require many decades for this critical problem to be eliminated."

MOBILIZING FOR ACTION [2]

One result of recent vigorous efforts to improve all levels and areas of education has been a surge of governmental and private action to wipe out illiteracy. More money and leadership are needed to get the movement rolling in high gear; but once the groundwork has been laid, the brunt of responsibility for the day-to-day operation is likely to fall upon public school administrators and their staffs. . . .

A good basic education is essential today for even minimum success in any field. The market for unskilled labor is declining steadily as new technology creates new jobs requiring new skills. The low pay and status of today's unskilled workers are encouraging many to seek better jobs.

To many illiterates, learning how to read and write is an important step to promotions or better jobs. For some, literacy is the answer to getting a job of any kind; for others, it means enjoyment, finally, of newspapers, books, and magazines and being able to write their own names. Also important is the self-respect and dignity it brings to people who once felt inferior and even humiliated because of their handicap.

Virtually all job-training programs . . . require that trainees be able to read and write. No longer can an apprentice learn how to use the tools of his trade through oral instruction or watching another man work. Textbooks, parts catalogs, and assembly manuals are standard today both for training and for day-to-day job activity.

The Bureau of the Census can prove a direct relationship between an individual's educational level and his occupation and

[2] From "The Illiterate American." *Overview.* 3:33-5. O. '62. Reprinted with permission from the October 1962 issue of *Overview* Magazine. Copyright 1962, Buttenheim Publishing Corporation.

income. It reports that, of employed males between thirty-five and fifty-four years of age with less than an eighth-grade education, 92 per cent earn less than $6,000 a year. . . . Moreover, workers with less than eighth-grade educations have 65 per cent of the incomes between $1,000 and $1,500 and 61 per cent of the incomes between $1,500 and $2,000.

Low-income, educationally deprived workers also have the highest unemployment rates, receive the bulk of public welfare aid, and comprise a substantial percentage of those rejected for military service. (During the Korean War, for example, one out of every eight recruits was rejected because of severe educational deficiencies; relatively few were feeble-minded.)

Who are these persons? Where do they live? What is being done about their plight?

Functional illiterates are concentrated in four main groups: (1) persons over forty years of age; (2) persons living on farms, especially Negroes; (3) persons with rural backgrounds who have moved to urban centers; and (4) migrant farm workers and other disadvantaged groups. Every year, their illiteracy is exacting a stiff price in wasted talent, lost wages, stifled ambition, and even weakened national security.

A National Problem

Although the South has the highest percentage of functional illiterates on a state-by-state basis, the problem is national, not regional, with the largest concentration of illiterates in urban centers across the nation. In the New York City area, for example, live nearly 800,000 illiterates (many of them Negro and Puerto Rican), comprising about 7 per cent of the population. Several other states have large numbers of functional illiterates. California has 505,000; Illinois, 365,000; Pennsylvania, 453,000; and Massachusetts, Indiana, Missouri, and Oklahoma each have more than 100,000.

Most literacy education is being carried out by public school adult education programs and by private groups and foundations. . . .

Meanwhile, the literacy education programs now in operation are nowhere near sufficient—either in quantity or quality—to meet current demand.

According to a report of the Office of Education, "Of the 15,200 school systems studied, only 4,840 have reported any type of adult education program, and of these, only 160, or 3.3 per cent, offer instruction in basic literacy education."

The report also points out that, of all adult education classes held last year by any group, only 1,430, or 1.1 per cent, were concerned with teaching basic literacy skills, and only about 47,000 persons received instruction.

Several of the key areas where literacy education has taken a foothold are Memphis, Tennessee; Dallas, Texas; New Orleans, Louisiana; Philadelphia, Pennsylvania; and northern Alabama through an eleven-county television network.

Educational TV: A Valuable Aid

In Memphis, headquarters of the Foundation for World Literacy, educational TV station WKNO began, six years ago, to broadcast a series of literacy education lessons taped by public school teachers in their spare time. Initial classes were so successful that an advanced course is now being broadcast to persons who have mastered the basic material.

In Dallas, the National Council of Jewish Women has developed a literacy training program for the 30,000 adults in the area who are unable to read or write. Chapter members have devoted thousands of hours to contacting students, providing teachers, and securing cooperation from schools and other public agencies.

In New Orleans, a project called LEARN (Literacy Education and Adult Reading for New Orleanians) has been set up to bring televised literacy education to the nearly 70,000 illiterates in the New Orleans area.

In Philadelphia, "Operation Alphabet," sponsored by the local school district, has produced a twenty-week series of television lessons in basic learning skills that are being broadcast by 100 commercial and ETV stations.

A Giant Step in Alabama

The most ambitious use of television for literacy education is being carried on in Alabama with the aid of a $66,000 NDEA [National Defense Education Act] grant. Using the only state-operated educational television network in the country, literacy education is being provided for an eleven-county area in northern Alabama where there are approximately 105,000 functional illiterates, including 19,000 persons who have never been to school.

The Laubach (picture-word association) method of teaching reading and writing is used in a program of ninety-eight lessons. [The system is named after F. C. Laubach, a missionary who originated the volunteer method of promoting literacy known as "each one, teach one."—Ed.] The lessons on TV are reinforced with group instruction by nonprofessional volunteer teachers with special training.

The televised lessons were launched with considerable publicity. Though only six hundred persons signed up for the original course, Miss Nell Peerson of the Foundation for World Literacy, director of the Alabama program, claims that "thousands more watched the lectures on their own." Supporting her statement is the fact that, in 1961-62, enrollment more than doubled (to 1,300), with many new students declaring their interest was stimulated by watching some of the previous year's lectures on television.

"We still are encountering a lot of difficulty getting illiterates to participate," Miss Peerson says. "They don't want to lose face with their friends and employers, and many are afraid the lessons will be too difficult for them." Although the program has not, as yet, effected a substantial reduction in the number of functional illiterates in Alabama, it does represent a giant step in the right direction.

More than ever before, the ability to read and write is a basic requirement for all who seek formal education, career success, or cultural development. In the words of the late Ambrose Caliver, former head of the USOE [United States Office of Education] adult education section and a pioneer in developing literacy education programs, "The best means a person has in making sound judgments is through the written word. It follows, therefore, that in our representative form of government, where each individual is sovereign, it is imperative that he be literate enough to exercise his sovereignty with intelligence and discretion."

ILLITERACY: THE KEY TO POVERTY [3]

There is a man in Chicago who dares think he has discovered the biggest cause of American poverty and how his city can begin to get rid of it. In fact, how any city can begin to get rid of it. His method—and this is not a flippancy—is as simple as teaching the ABC's.

Raymond M. Hilliard, the ruddy-faced, compassionate Director of Public Aid for Cook County, Illinois, recently was surprised to learn, after a long career of studying poverty, that most people who are extremely poor have in common a single, secret, crippling trait: They are virtually illiterate. He soon made other surprising discoveries. Impoverished illiterates and near-illiterates, no matter what their age, can be taught to read and write at insignificant cost ($5.50 a month), often in a few months, and many can be made employable and even employed. Perhaps most important, their education often leads to lifting the school interest and grades of their children. "This," says Hilliard, "is the most hopeful thing I've ever had hold of."

To appreciate the seeming hopelessness against which Hilliard pits his hope, one must realize how many Americans are poor and how poor they are. Not the $1.25-an-hour minimum-wage poor, but the empty-pocket poor. In addition to the tens of millions of miserably rewarded sharecroppers and scavengers,

[3] Article by Bernard Asbell, author of *Till the Robots Come. McCall's.* 91:96-7+.
F. '64. Reprinted by permission.

mop slingers and laundry sorters, and the job seekers and their
wives and youngsters who make do on unemployment-compensa-
tion checks, there are still $7\frac{1}{2}$ million souls who are even less
well off. More than the combined populations of Los Angeles,
Chicago, Pittsburgh, and Boston! Those are the Americans who
live by the grace of pubic welfare. Their parents were poor, and
unless something extraordinary is done rapidly, most of their
children will be poor. For the modern variety of "hard core"
poverty has something in common with the elegance and security
of established wealth. It is inherited.

Within months, one man rose from hopelessness to hope:
Sam Frost, a fifty-four-year-old ex-laborer with mighty shoulders
and a stony, solemn, awesomely proud jaw. Frost (I have changed
his name, but not his story) has fourteen children, the oldest
still in school. In 1959, after a thirty-four-year history of steady
employment, he was out of a job and could not for the life of
him find a new one. Uneasiness turned to fear, then to terrible
feelings of uselessness. Backaches and abdominal pains stabbed
at him. These are the occupational diseases of the unemployed;
they seem to vanish only under the miracle drug of opportunity.
Soon Frost reached the end of his downhill path: He and his
large family landed on relief.

Two years ago, Frost, like thousands of Chicagoans on relief,
was given a test in the three R's. Like many others, he failed to
show the formal learning of even a fifth-grade child. Soon he
was "requested" to go to school two nights a week and do
considerable homework in between (anyone refusing would for-
feit his relief checks, but almost everyone went gladly). In a
year and a half, Frost, an eager student, progressed from a near-
illiterate to a possessor of an eighth-grade certificate—and more.
His teacher, who volunteered to coach Frost after classes, feels
Sam is almost ready to take an achievement exam for a high-
school diploma.

That still is not the most remarkable of Frost's accomplish-
ments. Shell Oil Company admitted him to training as a gas-
station attendant and taught him how to fill out a shift foreman's

report, an intricate procedure for balancing all merchandise sold against money taken in. Frost mastered this better than some experienced foremen. Soon, several station owners jointly hired Frost to circulate from station to station, combining the figures from shifts into daily round-the-clock reports and finally into monthly reports. Also, he coaches station managers in better methods of record keeping. After more than five decades of ignorance, all this happened in less than two years.

Now Milwaukee, Baltimore, Newark, and other cities are also starting to send relief recipients to school. Like Chicago, they are teaching illiterates to read and write, others to qualify for grammar school and high school diplomas. These cities don't expect to find a Sam Frost behind every relief check; but they are convinced that only the thin walls of elementary schooling separate many good, useful men from productive employment of their native intelligence.

The intelligence exists, ready to be tapped, even though anyone able to read these words will find it hard—almost impossible —to appreciate the native cleverness an illiterate must possess to make his way through a wordy world. Just as a blind man "sees" with his ears and fingers, or a deaf man "hears" by staring at lips, the illiterate must "read" his way around.

Andrew Timmons has that special cleverness. Standing near the entrance of the public-housing project in Chicago where he lives with his wife and seven children, I pointed to a small wooden sign stuck into the dirt. It said, "Help us keep our lawn beautiful." I asked, "What does that sign say?" He replied confidently, "It says, 'Stay off the grass.'" I asked how he knew that. He said, "That's what those signs always say."

At thirty-seven, Timmons (that is not his real name) distinguishes one street from another by its houses, not its street signs. When he once had a job downtown as a car washer— the only job he could get in the past nine years—he was able to find his way home on the Cottage Grove bus because he knows it is number four ("I can read numbers"). When his wife sends him out for a can of tomato soup (which has only words on the label), he never brings home vegetable soup by mistake. He shops in the kind of grocery store where you ask for things, not where the customer selects from the shelf. Food is more costly there, but what can he do? Also, he has learned the ceremonial lies of the illiterate. Every culture has its ceremonial lies. Much as the educated suburbanite serves the best Scotch, so his guests won't know he's broke, Timmons sometimes tucks a newspaper under his arm, so his neighbors won't suspect he can't read. When people give him papers to fill out (sometimes job applications), he says, "I just got my hands dirty. Could you put this in your typewriter, and I'll tell you the answers?"

Timmons cannot, however, decipher a warning that says "Poison," a movie marquee, a big newspaper headline—or the tiny letters on newspapers' back pages that say "Help Wanted." He would be unable to compete for a job if he knew where to find one. Timmons, his wife, and his seven children are on relief, all of them supported by his fellow citizens who *do* know how to read and write.

Why didn't Timmons—and the rest of the ignorant poor—learn when they had the chance? The fact is that while other children were going to school, Timmons, a native citizen of the land of free education and equal opportunity, was not given the chance to go.

"Where I was raised," he told me (he had grown up in Jasper County, Mississippi), "hardly none of the kids ever went to school a day. Nobody from the school made you go. My grandfather—he raised me 'cause my mother died when I was seven—figured going to school wouldn't help me pick cotton any better, so why go? I hardly ever thought a thing about it till I was about fourteen and saw some kids in a store looking at magazines and things, and I wished I could do some of that. But it was too late."

Some did have the exceptional strength to defy such disadvantages; but even then, defeat was almost inevitable. One of Timmons' housing-project neighbors—also on relief—is a spunky woman in her fifties. I'll call her Maybelle Masters. Growing up

in Shelburne, Mississippi, she became determined not to mature
into an ignorant, helpless adult. At fifteen, she enrolled in the
first grade.

"Walking four miles in the mud was the only way to get to
school," she told me. "Lots of kids didn't go, because they didn't
have boots. On rainy days, the school would be closed, because
the rain would come down through the roof."

At the age of twenty—a fifth-grader—Maybelle got married
and quit school. The United States Census calls her literate
because she reported attending school for five years, the minimum
standard for "functional literacy." Yet she cannot read and
write. "When they ask me how long I went," says Mrs. Masters,
"I say five years, but the truth is I didn't go even eighteen months.
School was only open from January to April. Sometimes the
cotton wasn't all picked in January, so you couldn't start school
till the work was done. In April, the planting started. You
stopped going to school when the work started in the fields. So
maybe I went two months a year, maybe three."

Five "years" of schooling left her virtually as uneducated as
Andrew Timmons, who had had none.

Every large city is loaded with Andrew Timmonses, with
burdened, bewildered women and their ragged children, the
inheritors of what Hilliard calls "infectious ignorance." Chicago
is typical, with 270,000 on relief. Some are Southern Appalachian
mountaineers (sometimes said to be the only white Anglo-Saxon
Protestants who, as a class, are victims of discrimination and
deprivation). Some are Puerto Ricans, Mexicans, American Indians. But overwhelmingly they are Negroes who came from the
Deep South or whose parents did.

Much as America enjoys regarding itself as a nation of universal education, the 1960 census tells us that 8 million adults
over twenty-five—one out of every dozen—attended school less
than five years and are therefore labeled "functionally illiterate."
The statistic is far smaller than the truth. Selective Service
officials, for example, reject 22 per cent of draft registrants for
failing a simple mental test; in southern states, the percentage

of failures varies from 35 up to 56. These men aren't deliberate flunkers; the test is mined with devices for trapping malingerers. Testing officers say that the young men fail mainly because they can't read the questions.

In Oklahoma City, a meat-packer and two unions agreed jointly to retrain 170 workers displaced by new machines. They found 110—or 65 per cent—too uneducated "to show promise of benefiting from training." More bluntly, the workers couldn't read and do simple figuring. In Michigan, a group of 761 unemployed were tested for retraining; 515—or 68 per cent—failed. In Chicago, 4,500 on relief were tested; 1,900 were unable to read well enough to pass.

Hardly any jobs remain for such ignorant laborers. The road-gang worker has been replaced by the bulldozer and grading machine, operated by men of training. Even the janitor is no longer a mindless floor sweeper. He must operate cleaning machines, study a manual for making repairs, read instructions for careful mixing of cleaning agents. In the modern restaurant, a short-order cook must read scribbled orders from waitresses.

Illiteracy, therefore, is no longer an unfortunate statistic. It has become a serious national threat.

Hilliard, the Chicago welfare chief, started to be aware of this fact in January 1959. He was disturbed by a chart on his desk and called in his energetic research director, Deton J. Brooks, Jr. A recession had just ended. Employment was picking up. According to past experience, relief rolls should be declining. But they kept rising. Why was this happening?

Hilliard and Brooks decided on an intensive study of a large, crowded, poverty-stricken neighborhood called Woodlawn, where 25 per cent of all households were on relief. One of their findings seemed to tower in significance above all others. According to the census, 6.6 per cent of relief recipients had five years of schooling or less. But standard tests in the three R's revealed that 51 per cent of the able-bodied adults were unable to read and write at a fifth-grade level. The remainder, who tested higher, were so little above functional illiteracy that the difference hardly mattered. Nearly all were too uneducated for the simplest jobs in the modern labor market.

"Here, then," said Hilliard, reporting his findings to a convention of welfare officials, "is the major cause of today's poverty. Here is the reason for the high cost of relief. Punishing these people for their poverty won't help. Badgering them with investigations, violating their small rights of privacy, condemning them for alleged immorality, putting them in jail, calling them loafers and idlers and cheats and frauds, which few of them are, will avail nothing. . . . These only divert attention from real solutions."

As a real solution, Hilliard set about to teach fifty thousand relief recipients to read and write better. By last December, the eight thousand most urgently needing education were going to school, but money was lacking for the rest. The Chicago Board of Education has been footing the entire cost, providing classrooms and paying regular schoolteachers $4.50 an hour for the two evening sessions per week that classes are held. To carry these costs, the Board of Education siphoned off money earmarked for Americanizing the foreign-born; later, Hilliard obtained Federal and state funds to finance the classes.

The biggest initial problem was trying to arrange baby-sitters to free mothers for school. If women's organizations were prepared to offer such help, Hilliard believes, they would make a unique contribution to helping families rid themselves of poverty. Lacking such help, welfare caseworkers undertook the huge job of arranging mutual baby-sitting among the student mothers. Last summer, when classes were changed to daytime to save custodial costs in school buildings, the baby-sitting problem became so difficult that many of the sessions had to be canceled.

Considering how many schemes for teaching literacy to adults have sprung up, one would think the techniques were down to a science. In Yakima, Washington, the LARK (Literacy for Adults and Related Knowledge) Foundation has organized classes as far east as Michigan. In St. Louis, the Adult Education Council has aggressively sought to educate illiterates. Indiana Central College started a course for teaching teachers of illiterates. Daily TV instruction programs—one series produced in Philadelphia, another in Memphis—have been lent to other cities, in the hope that illiterates will tune in. But everywhere, teachers are groping for effective teaching methods.

This came as a shock to Robert L. Dixon, a junior high school teacher supervising some Chicago welfare classes. He recalls the first orientation meeting of several hundred teachers. "Before you ask what textbooks you are to use," the speaker said, "let me tell you that we have none. We know that the Little Red Hen won't do for adults, but we don't know what *will* do. Your students are not like immigrants who want to learn to speak English. For most of your students, English is the only language they know. This challenge is new. We will have to find our way by experimenting."

Dixon faced his first class, composed entirely of Negroes like himself, with uneasiness. His chief tools were a piece of chalk and a blackboard. His twenty students sat with pencils poised over notebooks. There were two women for each man. Young people far outnumbered the elderly.

First, I wondered how much they know about the world [Dixon told me]. Next, I wondered how much they know that I don't know. I had to keep reminding myself that they had rich experiences I know nothing about. One had been a paint mixer, one a drill-press operator, a few housewives and mothers, each with full lives, some longer than mine. I had to remind myself not to lump them together with a simple label like "illiterate."

Then I began to wonder how much they think I know, what they imagined book learning really is. This made me wonder—and this was the most troubling of all—how much they expected of me.

His students came with uneasiness, too.

"I wondered," said Eddie O'Brien, a father of twelve, "how much education a man needed so he could get himself a job, and how long it would take. I was forty-two already and didn't have much time."

O'Brien took it as no joke when Dixon distributed play money and set up a shelf full of commodities for "sale." As pupils "bought" things, the teacher spun a line of talk, meanwhile shortchanging each of his customers. They were first embarrassed, then stunned as Mr. Dixon revealed the simple ways in which salesmen can fleece the uneducated.

These ways had cost O'Brien his last job. For seven years, he had worked for a baking company, stacking baked goods as they came down automatic conveyors and sweeping crumbs from the floor. He took home $84 a week.

"I wanted to be like the rest of the people," O'Brien told me. "I bought a used car, some furniture we needed, a TV set, clothes for the kids. Those salesmen, they always kept telling me it wasn't hard, just a dollar down, a dollar a week. Before I knew it, I was caught in the trick bag."

The "trick bag" had many hidden pockets. If educated people are often swindled for overlooking fine print, how easy to skin someone unable to read even big print. One day, a lawyer informed O'Brien he could be saved from his creditors only by claiming personal bankruptcy. The lawyer would gladly arrange this for $300. Payments would be easy: $100 down, $40 a month. When the fourth payment for the lawyer fell due, O'Brien was unable to pay. Thus he forfeited $220 he had already paid, and the lawyer abandoned the case. O'Brien's creditors descended on the baking company to claim slices of his wages, and he was fired for "excessive wage assignments," a phrase well known in slum districts. Soon his family was on relief.

Students like Eddie O'Brien come eager to learn. After the first embarrassment at being exposed to friends as uneducated, many are seized with a desire to spell their children's names. They recite the names to the teacher and become absorbed in the magical process of copying down the letters—sometimes the first meaningful syllables they have ever written. One woman, after three months of tutelage, brought her teacher an elaborate chocolate cake. She carried it proudly and announced, "I got a book all about cooking and *read* how to make it."

Eddie O'Brien describes his sense of achievement differently: "I feel like a caged bird that all at once got out." His escape has indeed been dramatic, for he escaped into the exhilarating world of self-dependence and self-respect. O'Brien is now averaging $450 a month driving a taxi. He is one of the most successful of almost five hundred drivers lifted from the literacy classes and relief rolls and trained for jobs by the Yellow Cab Company. Once they had demonstrated that they could read street signs, they were taught Chicago's house-numbering system, the location of the city's seventy-eight most important buildings, and how to fill out trip reports. Also, they were given special training in meeting the public—and how to buy sensibly on the installment plan. Now, Yellow Cab expects to train a thousand relief recipients, possibly more.

The Chicago Urban League brought the Yellow Cab story to the Shell Oil Company because major oil companies have been troubled by a shortage of high-grade gas-station attendants. Sales are lost by employees who don't seem to care, and the man who meets the customer can make or break the reputation of his company.

With trepidation, Shell undertook to train a group of men from the literacy classes. Strange things happened. In tests for spelling, for example, men continued to have trouble with words like "which," but racked up high scores in technical words like "detergency" and "differential." Company officials accepted this as a surprising sign that the men were burning late lamps. It helped destroy company fears that "reliefers" were natural loafers. Still, the company was skeptical. Yet two months after the men went to work, seven out of thirty-five had already been promoted to shift foremen, taking charge of men who had been on the job a year or more. Station owners reported that the new men were among their best employees. The training program is now permanent.

While the star trainee at Shell, Sam Frost, who became the roving bookkeeper, was working furiously to learn, his eighteen-year-old son, a recent high school dropout, began talking about going back to school, and his grammar school children headed for their homework whenever Daddy did.

Commissioner Hilliard is convinced that educating mothers is equally important. Half the homes in Negro slum neighborhoods are headed by women, most of them abandoned early in marriage. Hilliard's research director, Deton Brooks, explains:

In a matriarchal structure, women transmit the culture. If the woman is illiterate, she transmits the values, the images of an illiterate's world. This is extremely dangerous, for the future of these children and the society that may soon have to support them as illiterate adults.

Extending this reasoning, Hilliard is convinced that literacy, classes strike at the roots of broken homes. He concludes:

You can see a straight line operating from illiteracy to illegitimacy. The American culture teaches all men—even Negro men segregated from the main culture—that a father's job is to be a provider. The man who had been abandoned by his father and in turn abandons his children is convinced he can never succeed as a good American father. Where's his chance to provide? From the day he takes his vows, he knows he can't fulfill his function, that his manhood has been taken away, that his marriage is doomed, and that the insecurity of his woman has begun.

Instead of heaping more contempt on this man, let's look for ways that will let him stay at home. Let's give him at least the meagerest education, to help him find a decent job at a decent wage, and give him some assurance that he won't be the first one fired because of his color. Then you'll start to see a downslide in the illegitimacy rate. That's how far you can extend the possible results of something as simple as teaching the ABC's.

THE NEW LOST GENERATION: JOBLESS YOUTH [4]

The computers which have tabulated the Federal reports on youth unemployment might have been programed by Emile Zola rather than IBM. Their statistics are the quantification of a social tragedy, the description of a generation lost beyond Hemingway's imagining.

In February 1963, President Kennedy pointed to the ominous convergence of high dropout rates, chronic youth unemployment

[4] From article by Michael Harrington, author of *The Other America: Poverty in the United States*. New York *Times Magazine*. p 13+. My. 24 '64. © 1964 by The New York Times Company. Reprinted by permission.

and an economy which was eliminating unskilled and semiskilled jobs. The situation, he concluded, was "critical." A year later, Lyndon B. Johnson's poverty message described "the young man or woman who grows up without a decent education, in a broken home, in a hostile and squalid environment, in ill health or in the face of racial injustice"—and declared "that young man or woman is often trapped in a life of poverty." More bluntly, Secretary of Labor Willard Wirtz has said the failure to come to grips with this problem is a form of "economic suicide."

But perhaps the most poignant index to the chaos of an entire subgeneration in American life was given by the Administration when it explained what it hoped to accomplish under the education programs proposed in the projected Conservation Camps. These will seek to raise the young volunteers up to a minimum reading level of the seventh grade. And they will literally undertake to teach these young citizens how to speak their own language—"to be understood in employment and other conventional situations, and to understand directions."

What is the dimension of this problem in which young Americans must be federally schooled in order "to understand directions"? What is the look of the faces behind the figures? And where is there a basis for hope, both for them and for the society which bred them?

In the Administration's presentation of the Economic Opportunity Act of 1964, one finds this frank statement:

In October of 1963, there were 730,000 young men and women between the ages of sixteen and twenty-one who were both out of school and out of work. This figure had increased 22 per cent in a one-year period. But this unemployment figure for a specific week in October does not tell the whole story. Many others are employed only in low-paying dead-end jobs which are beneath their potential abilities. . . .
Left to itself, the problem will multiply. . . . If the current trends continue, in five years we will have almost 1.5 million unemployed youth—without education or training, without jobs and without a future.

There are Government figures which state the crisis even more broadly. During the sixties, there will be some 26 million new entrants into the labor force in consequence of the post-World War II baby boom. Of these, it is estimated that 7.5 million will not have finished high school—and 2.3 million will be under the eighth-grade level. This vast influx of the untrained will take place in a technological setting which will probably require the minimum of a high school diploma as the prerequisite for a moderately decent job.

But it is not necessary to speculate on the future; the present is plain enough. Between May 1962 and May 1963, according to the House committee which reported on the Manpower Development and Training Act, the labor force grew by 1.2 million, while jobs increased only by 900,000. "Nearly the entire impact of this rise in joblessness was felt by the sixteen-to-nineteen-year-old youth in the labor market," the committee reported. "Their unemployment rate rose to over 20 per cent, approximately four times the rate of the adult labor force."

The statistics are conservative. To qualify as officially unemployed, a youth must be in the labor market looking for a job. Yet, according to Labor Secretary Wirtz, there are now more than 300,000 young people who are not in school, not at work and not looking for work. They are simply floating in the society; they have fallen off our misery charts. It goes, almost without saying, that a disproportionate number of this grim lost generation of the sixties is "nonwhite." Yet it is not true that the majority is Negro or belongs to other racial minorities. The House Labor Committee noted that, in 1962, 57 per cent of the nonwhite youths and 28 per cent of the whites between twenty and twenty-four years old were dropouts. Given the numerical dominance of whites in the nation, this adds up to a problem which is, by a majority, white.

Another important fact about the young poor is that they are largely the children of the middle-aged poor and the grandchildren of the aging poor. The President's Economic Report spells out the hereditary character of American poverty in some detail. Of the families now defined as poor, 64 per cent are headed by a person with less than an eighth-grade education; and

67 per cent of the fathers of these family heads were without a grade-school diploma.

In the Department of Labor's brilliantly developed and shocking report, "One Third of a Nation," a study of Selective Service rejectees yielded the same result. About a quarter of the young Americans who appeared before draft boards were rejected because they were not up to the seventh-grade level. Four out of five were dropouts, a third were unemployed and a high percentage were second- or third-generation relief cases.

Indeed, the social chances of the dropout and the teen-aged unemployed have become so institutionalized that the Government had to make a frank admission of its failure in even reaching the most desperate among them in the Manpower Development and Training Program.

When this effort began, it was assumed that the great problem would be that of job training. But then it was realized, as a House committee put it, that ". . . when available job opportunities are discovered and the necessary programs devised, the vast majority of the unemployed cannot pass entrance examinations. In fact, large numbers cannot even be tested, since they are unable to read and write."

So there emerged the incredible fact that, nationally, only one out of eight among the unemployed was even qualified to take advantage of hope when it was offered. This will certainly be true of the 2.3 million youth without an eighth-grade education who will enter the economy during this decade. It is why Sargent Shriver [whom President Johnson selected in August 1964 to head the nation's antipoverty program] must propose to teach seventh-grade levels of reading and simple spoken English in the training camps. And these are the figures that make the Administration's estimate of a possible million and a half teen-aged unemployed in five years a conservative guess.

Finally, these figures require computation in social, as well as economic, terms. The evidence is overwhelming that youthful hopelessness expresses itself in violence and aimless acts of desperation. In New Haven, for instance, a recent study reported that 18 per cent of the high-school graduates and 48 per cent of the school dropouts had one or more juvenile arrests. As Abraham Ribicoff testified to the House when he was Secretary of Health, Education and Welfare in 1961, juvenile delinquency among the impoverished youth is not so much individual lawlessness as it is "a system of beliefs and values with a strong and stable tradition of its own."

"Nobody Knows My Name" author James Baldwin called a collection of his essays. When one speaks of these young people as individuals rather than as the raw data of statistics, it is probably true that nobody knows *their* names. Dropouts literally disappear from public view. That is one of the reasons why the Administration says it needs Selective Service—a comprehensive and legally compulsive mechanism—rather than the school system as a way to obtain an introduction to some of the young people it seeks to help. Beyond that, if it is necessary to teach the youth in the conservation camps to talk to the rest of society, who will teach society to speak to them?

I talked to a group of three Negroes, all of them unemployed dropouts. They corroborated more contradictory explanations of their behavior than one could have believed possible; which is to say, I did not feel that I had understood them at all.

"They're living on their wits and their kicks," a civil rights leader had said to me about this kind of youth, lost in the city. They were. When I talked to them, they were high (though on liquor, not narcotics). They were restless, shadow-boxing, given to bursts of laughter and comment—energetic like adolescents generally, but more catlike than gawkish. In this persona, their talk was of girls, drinking, fighting, the life of the streets.

If the conversation had stopped there, they could have been defined simply: as filling up their futureless spare time with a desperate, aimless sensualism, living by petty crime and headed nowhere.

Then the talk turned a corner and the three were different people. Edgar Friedenberg, the author of *The Vanishing Adolescent,* has argued that the slum kid is the "last aristocrat," "ignorant, often emotionally disturbed to the point of paranoia, dangerous when threatened and parochial. . . . But he has the qualities of his defects: forthrightness, a capacity for real human commitment, more spontaneity. . . ."

The three young men suddenly exhibited these virtues. They had a pride in having borne their miseries, a camaraderie. (On a much more sophisticated level, one hears Negroes in the civil rights movement, sometimes when among friends, use the word "nigger" as an act of defiance against the white world which thus branded them, but also as a stubborn assertion of the community which the brand has evoked.) At this point, they were contemptuous of the attempts being made to rescue them. The whites would certainly do nothing but talk; and anyway, who wanted a place in an office or a factory? There was value enough in a Harlem street.

Their final mood was the most explicitly sociological, and the most ambiguous. In part, it corroborated the wisdom of the song "Officer Krupke" in *West Side Story:*—that some, at least, at the bottom of the society have learned the social-scientific, psycho-analytic, welfare-state clichés about themselves. And in part, it reflected the impact of the civil rights movement in the ghettos of the North. I was not sure whether I was hearing what they thought I wanted them to say, or what they felt—or perhaps both.

Their plight, they agreed, was due to the fact that society was organized against them. They had failed in school, not out of a lack of ability, but because there had been no money at home, no space, no possibility of study. They, in their late teens, were already victims. Maybe politics and the movement would change some things; maybe the Government had been forced into being serious; maybe there was some hope.

And yet, it is a paradox that the very viciousness of American racism has provoked a certain sophistication in the most exploited single group in the society. The Negro unemployed, young and old, have a leadership, a movement; the March on Washington was for jobs and freedom.

Thus, the three Negroes contrasted sharply with some white teen-agers in another city who seemed destined to become dropouts. (It is one of the saddest things about this social underworld that any reasonable person can make a fair guess about the fate hanging over a thirteen- or fourteen-year-old long before it happens.) They were already well behind in school, and it was doubtful that any of them would see a grade school diploma. Yet they did not have the utter cynicism of the older Negro youth, perhaps because their membership in the racial majority allowed them illusions which Harlem simply cannot afford. At least insofar as we communicated with one another, they persisted in dreaming of adult careers that required college degrees. . . .

Given these massive social determinants of the problem, and its delicate human dimension, is there any reason to think that such youth can be rescued?

The experience of the past is affirmative. Every time there has been a shooting war in the twentieth century, with its concomitant full employment in the advanced nations, hundreds of thousands of "unemployables" have suddenly been discovered to have viable skills. From this point of view, the creation of a full-employment economy is a fundamental prerequisite for doing anything about this new lost generation. A significant number of students, the Government has discovered, drop out of school, not because they want to, but because their parents cannot afford to have them off the labor market. Some of these dropouts become unemployed because they are in the scramble for cheap, unskilled jobs. Federal support for such children—perhaps through some form of the "GI Bill" in the war against poverty—and full employment would save many.

Predictably, such a development would rescue the best, the most educated and motivated, of the unemployed youth. But, as the figures make clear, there are other millions of young people who will enter the economy during this decade who will probably be immune even to the advantages of full employment. (The 2.3 million with less than an eighth-grade education certainly fall into this category; so do many of the 7.5 million without high school diplomas.)

It is to this problem that the Administration has addressed two new programs in the antipoverty package: the Job Corps (both the Conservation and the Training Camps) for 30,000 to 40,000 young people in its first phase; and the work-training program (in which Washington will, essentially, subsidize some state, municipal and nonprofit work for those in school), to extend to 200,000 youth. Both ideas involve special training and education for those at a "structural disadvantage in the American economy. . . .

Under present conditions, there is no reason to believe that a full-employment economy is around the corner. The tax cut may reduce the jobless rate to 5 per cent; it could even bring it down to the 4 per cent predicted by some of the more optimistic in Washington. But a work situation that could bring these youth back into the society will require more than that. As proposed by the AFL-CIO, it will certainly take a $2 billion investment in accelerated public works in the immediate future; and beyond that, a more basic public commitment to meet the housing, school, hospital, transportation and other needs not only of the poor but of the rest of the society as well.

The Administration has made a beginning, which is in itself a positive accomplishment. It may take the President and Mr. Shriver a while to educate the people on the extent and the critical character of problems like those of the dropouts and the unemployed youth. But time presses and once that is done, much larger steps will have to be taken.

For, typically in this America of midcentury, the Government has admitted the existence of problems it has not yet proposed even to touch. The first installment in the Training Camps will be for some 40,000—and one quarter of the Selective Service rejectees cannot read at a seventh-grade level. There will be over 2 million young people in this decade, the majority of whom are yet to appear, without a grade school diploma. Even under conditions of full employment, where will they fit?

As it now stands, the Secretary of Labor has a broad authority to undertake studies of the labor market. Yet there is no effective "early warning system" for automation, such as he has proposed. Without a knowledge of the job needs of the future, of those occupations going into decline and those coming to the fore, it will be next to impossible to develop a rational education and training system for these youth. Among other things, the American prejudice against planning (an irrationality already discarded by most European conservatives) will have to be dropped.

All of these proposals clearly require large changes in American thinking, yet they are necessary to meet the problem of youth as America has defined it. And beyond, the figures suggest that if these young people are to have meaningful lives, perhaps the nation will have to make some new definitions of work (are not the full-time officers of a nonbopping club in the slums "social workers" of a sort?) and of pay (going to school is probably the most productive activity a young person can undertake in this society and, as such, could be compensated for).

In any case, given the Zolaesque underworld of the impoverished youth described by the computers, the Economic Opportunity Act of 1964 is a praiseworthy point of departure. It is, to quote one of the late President Kennedy's maxims, that necessary first step in a journey of a thousand miles.

THE UNPRODUCTIVES [5]

In this land of "free, public education for all" there are still 44 million citizens fourteen years old and over who would fail to pass as modest an educational requirement for modern citizenship as completion of the ninth grade. There are 67 million Americans who have not completed high school; 2 million more who never went to school at all.

Each one of the individuals counted in these millions is "undereducated" by almost any standard. Each one represents a drain on the productive economy of our country and a potential weakening of our democratic tradition.

[5] From "The Cost of Adult Undereducation," by Robert A. Luke, director, Division of Adult Education Service, National Education Association, and executive secretary, National Association of Public School Adult Educators. *NEA Journal.* 45:428-9. O. '56. Reprinted by permission.

The costs to society of supporting the undereducated adult are of both economic and political concern. Just as costly, but more poignant, are the costs to the undereducated adult himself in terms of his own personal frustrations and bewilderments.

He is the last to be hired and the first to be fired. He must contend daily with problems of which educated people are never aware. Because his skills and personal resurces are limited, the illiterate and undereducated person has little chance to solve his problems by self-help. The chances are great that he faces an old age of dependency unlightened by memories of past achievement and unrelieved by satisfactions of intellectual and spiritual insight.

All kinds of remedial and welfare services must be called upon to assist the undereducated person. He must be aided in times of economic recession. His low earning capacity makes it necessary for the community to bear some of the costs of maintaining him and his family during times of severe illness. . . .

Of all the losses caused by undereducation, the loss to responsible citizenship is the greatest of all. If a well-informed citizenry is a prerequisite of a functioning democracy, then lack of education is a continuing threat to our way of life.

If the American way is to continue to attract mankind as a way of living in freedom, it must simultaneously remain ahead in the skills of production and commerce, and in political and cultural advancement. This will call for adequate industrial and social research; for informed political discussion; and for an educated, wise, versatile, and productive citizenry.

A few mental giants will not be enough. Millions of John and Mary Does are also needed, men and women with the necessary skills and personal resources to solve the problems and measure up to the responsibilities of democratic citizenship in an industrial society.

The task of meeting the needs of the undereducated adult falls squarely into the hands of the teachers of adults. This is not to suggest that the existing adult-education programs of the public schools should be limited to the undereducated or that they are so limited at present. Rather it is to say that such programs do represent a stable and experienced educational service equipped to serve individuals whose schooling is limited.

At the present time, about half of the adult-education programs offered by public school systems are for those people who are either trying to catch up on the education they missed in earlier years or who are seeking economic advancement. Specifically, about 17 per cent of the people who take adult education classes offered by public schools are enrolled in vocational classes. Another 14 per cent are completing high school education, and 9 per cent are engaged in elementary studies or Americanization courses.

Together these three groups of enrollees account for 40 per cent of all adults using the urban public school education service. If we add to them the large proportion of rural enrollees who are following practical courses in agriculture, the figure of 50 per cent is developed for all adult education students who could be assumed to be engaged in some form of remedial or vocational education.

These facts show the extent to which the undereducated now have assistance from the adult educator. Unfortunately, this service is not available throughout the nation. . . .

If adult education is to play its part in assisting the undereducated to better themselves economically and fulfill themselves as people, the service of adult education must be made available to all. This can only be done if considerable funds from state sources, as well as from local school districts, become available.

This is now the practice in ten states. In the local communities of these "state-aid" states, the average expenditure for adult education is 91 cents per person. Of this total, only 35 cents per person comes from state funds; but the amount of extra adult education that this 35 cents can buy is truly remarkable! In these states, classes for adults reach three times as many people as in states without this assistance.

In New York State, the additional funds from state sources caused an even more spectacular increase in the extent and range

of program offerings. From 1945 to 1953, the number of enrollments in adult education activities offered by local school districts
in New York State increased over fifteen times.

Because all states are eligible to receive some Federal money
to aid in providing vocational classes for adults, the largest single
concentration of adult education enrollment for the country as a
whole is in vocational education. This fact is a striking illustra-
tion of the stimulating effect which supplementary funds have
upon adult education programs even in states where no state aid
is given. . . .

If the needs of all people for adult education are to be met, a
vast expansion of adult education under public school auspices is
required. And, if this expansion occurs, the schools must be
prepared to face new challenges in addition to those they already
have. Since no one is likely to suggest compulsory adult attendance laws, other methods must be devised to draw adults
into the adult education workshop of the public schools.

In addition, greater attention must be given to the selection
and training of teachers of adults. School facilities must undergo
some modification. School districts must turn to full-time di-
rectors of adult education to assist in working out these and
other problems.

How much will it cost? In 1953, the cost of public school
adult education amounted to 76 cents for every person over
eighteen years old in the population. This was equal to only 1.3
per cent of all expenditures for public schools. Of the total cost
of $79 million, about $22 million came from Federal funds
through the Veterans Administration, and another $6 million
came from aid for vocational education. . . .

If we are to try to overcome the educational deficit of many
of our citizens, we must at least double our over-all expenditures
for public school adult education. Most of the money should
come from states which now invest almost nothing toward the
elimination of the great social waste of undereducation. It is
encouraging to note that the number of states appropriating funds
for adult education is increasing and so is the number of states

where consultants in adult education are made available to local school districts.

All over America, responsible men and women are increasingly responding to the necessity of doing something about undereducation. Many agencies throughout the country are participating, but the basic responsibility and opportunity logically belong to the public schools. In practically every community there is a public school with the personnel and facilities required to improve the vocational skills of adults, to eliminate illiteracy, and to help all those who lack a high school education to obtain it.

It should be stressed that adult education is as vital to the Ph.D. or the "senior citizen" as to the undereducated person we have defined in this article. Therefore, nothing said in this article is intended to de-emphasize the importance of the public schools' providing a liberal arts education for adults or educational programs designed to aid effective and informed citizen participation on the part of all adults.

However, at the same time that these areas of adult education are being developed and expanded, adult education must continue to be made available to all those who were undereducated in their youth.

A DEMOCRACY AND ITS CITIZENS [6]

One of the major blocks to literacy and progress is the fact that most people do not understand the functioning of their own society. The countries of Western Europe and the United States do not realize that their economic advancement is rooted in their substantial investments to improve the quality of their population, particularly through education. Most people in the United States have attributed their economic progress to the machine. Understandably, foreigners have also equated the wellsprings of U.S. economic progress with advances in technology—overlooking the fact that only men could invent, develop, operate, and maintain the vast technological equipment.

[6] From "10,000,000 U.S. Illiterates," by Eli Ginzberg, author of a number of books on education and undereducation. *Américas*. 10:6-10. N. '58. Reprinted from *Americas*, monthly magazine published by the Pan American Union in English, Spanish and Portuguese.

Paradoxically, a high percentage of literates does not make it easier to combat illiteracy. Business enterprises, for example, tend to adjust their activities to the prevailing level of skill of the men and women whom they are able to hire. Today, since the overwhelming proportion of the population is literate, U.S. business would be loath to hire anyone, no matter how talented, who could not fill out the employment forms and read or write the other basic records on which its operations are based. Even the night watchman must be able to set down the time he inspects each section of the plant.

An outstanding characteristic of the U.S. economy has been the mobility of its population—workers go wherever opportunity calls. But an illiterate will be fearful of losing touch with those back home, and of even trying for a job in a new location where everyone else can read and write. As for the efforts of government and voluntary agencies to attract new industry to depressed areas, they will fail wherever the labor force has nothing to offer but brawn. . . .

A different but related problem is presented by the Puerto Rican immigrants on the eastern seaboard and to a lesser extent by the Mexicans, especially in the Southwest. The number of Puerto Ricans is already sufficiently large in New York City to represent a significant factor in the city's labor supply, particularly in many service trades and light manufacturing industry. If Puerto Ricans should continue to immigrate in considerable numbers, as appears likely, their successful integration into the economy and the larger society will largely depend on the rate at which they become literate in English. The better jobs will be closed to them until they do; nor can their children take full advantage of the educational and other opportunities. Not long ago a truant officer who asked a Puerto Rican mother why she did not send her children to school was told that she had no idea she was required to. . . .

At a time when people are increasingly sensitive to the evils of discrimination, special weight must be given to the role of literacy in its eradication, especially since minority groups, particularly Negroes and immigrants, comprise a disproportionately high percentage of the illiterate population. Some time ago the United States Government encouraged a large number of Navaho Indians to leave their reservation because it could not support their rapidly expanding population. But illiteracy soon proved to be a major hurdle to their integration into the larger community. The outside world was twice as threatening to the illiterate Indian as to the one who had had contact with it through books and who knew that his ability to read and write [would] make his adjustment on the outside much easier. Moreover, illiteracy actually contributes to discrimination: to many among the native white population, their own literacy supports their conviction that they are better than the black-, red-, or brown-skinned man who is unlettered. . . .

The crucial role parents play in the upbringing of their children—in every society, the stable agricultural as well as the dynamic industrial—underscores the importance of trying to eradicate illiteracy among adults. A society that educates its youth and leaves its elders to flounder risks serious troubles; by widening the gulf between the generations, it encourages the young to denigrate the wisdom and worth of older people. While this may fit in with the aims of a leadership seeking to break with tradition, there is the danger that the break will become so abrupt that uncontrollable forces will be unleashed. Yet the more rapidly a society is changing, the more difficult the parents' task, since the knowledge they acquired from their own parents is not adequate for their children.

Take health, for example. Rapid changes in medicine have revolutionized the care of infants and children within the past half century. Nowadays, a baby born healthy is almost certain to live to adulthood unless he is killed in an accident. The most widely disseminated publications of the United States Government are its pamphlets on infant and child care; in United States homes, Dr. Spock's handbook on the same subject has surpassed the Bible in popularity. But such literature is useless for illiterate parents. Some years ago an experiment was undertaken in the region around Tuskegee, Alabama, in which medical services were offered at minimum cost to a group of Negroes who had had little prior contact with modern culture. Taking advantage of them meant that they would be healthier and live longer. Yet many could not be weaned from their reliance on folk medicine because, among other reasons, their illiteracy had cut them off from and made them suspicious of the dynamic world outside.

Or take guidance. Among the most important challenges every child faces is to profit from the schooling available to him and to choose wisely from the alternative career opportunities open to him. But no child can do this alone, and illiterate parents can hardly serve as either models or advisers. . . .

Regrettably, no modern state can close its eyes to the need, if war comes, to be ready to mobilize its resources quickly and effectively. In both World Wars, the United States entered late. Fortunately, our allies held the enemy at bay until we could mobilize our strength. But in this nuclear age no large nation will ever again have several years' grace after the outbreak of a major conflict. Current defense plans provide for warning systems in terms of minutes.

A nation concerned about the state of its military preparedness must act in times of peace to raise the quality of its population; after the outbreak of hostilities will be too late. The Congress of the United States has long recognized the important role in defense of stand-by plants and the stockpiling of strategic materials. It has yet to appreciate fully the equally important role of investing adequately in the nation's human resources so that in an emergency each man will be able to perform with maximum competence.

Currently the Armed Forces accept no illiterates or borderline illiterates and, finding themselves with too many men of limited skills and learning potential, have asked Congress for permission for even further restrictions. The more complex the weapons, the greater the educational demands. We have here the counterpart of the civilian economy, in which the unskilled man, whose only advantage is his physical strength, is being squeezed out.

So we face the broader question: Can a democratic society function effectively in the contemporary world unless its citizens are literate? How can an individual discharge the responsibilities of citizenship unless he can meet the call to arms, unless he can inform himself on the issues of the day and express his opinions with respect to them? How can a free press, on which a democratic society depends, flourish without a literate populace?

PROBLEMS AND PROSPECTS [7]

Lack of schooling results in lower earning capacity, higher rates of unemployment, more dependence on public welfare, higher rejections for military service, and insufficient literary skills for vocational training and retraining.

It has been shown that a direct relationship exists between an adult's educational attainment, his occupation, and consequently his earnings. The amount of formal schooling a person has received is a major determinant of his occupational group. For example, among men eighteen years old and older in 1959, 60 per cent of the college graduates were in professional and technical fields and about 20 per cent were managers, officials, or proprietors. Among men who completed high school, but did not go beyond, a majority were found in three occupational groups—craftsmen; operatives; and managers, officials, or proprietors. Those with some high school, but lacking four completed years, and men who finished elementary school, but who did not go on to high school, were most likely to have become operatives or craftsmen. Those with lesser amounts of education were most usually found—when employed at all—in farm service and in unskilled laboring jobs. . . .

The story of illiteracy during World War II is very well known. Nearly 400,000 illiterates were accepted and trained for military service. Another 300,000 illiterates—equal to twenty army divisions—were rejected completely. During the Korean

[7] From "Undereducation in our American Society," by Edward Warner Brice, director, Adult Education Branch, Office of Education, United States Department of Health, Education and Welfare. *Illinois Education*. 25:387-9. My. '63. Reprinted by permission.

War more than 19 per cent of all recruits were rejected from military service on grounds of educational deficiencies. Many of these men could learn, but overcoming their previous educational deprivations was costly and time-consuming. Draft registrants rejected for "mental reasons," including educational deficiencies, ranged from 56 to 39 per cent in the four highest states. Ten other states had rejection rates exceeding 21 per cent. There is some cause for general alarm over the fact that from July 1950, to September 1961, more than 900,000 draft registrants out of 6 million examined were rejected on the basis of a mental test alone. This was almost as many as were disqualified on medical grounds. It was clear from the record that low educational attainment was the largest single reason for rejection.

In 1962 it was dramatically outlined that our technology is outpacing our human skills on the one hand and our social attitudes on the other. Too many young people are entering the labor force without sufficient training to land jobs. Too many Negroes are unemployable because of educational deficiencies. The Government's huge effort to upgrade worker skills got under way and completed its first year of manpower retraining in depressed areas under the Area Redevelopment Act of 1961. And last August [1962] it began the task of retraining 400,000 unemployed and underemployed Americans during the next three years under the Manpower Development and Retraining Act of 1962. So far in most places the retraining effort has been fairly successful in the proportion of trainees placed in jobs. But this program has uncovered a disturbing condition that goes to the very root of our educational system. The number of unemployed academically qualified for retraining is discouragingly small. In one project only 97 or 2.4 per cent finished courses out of 3,500 semiskilled job applicants originally screened. Official reports from West Virginia indicate that fully 50 per cent of the state's unemployed are functionally illiterate. There is a growing feeling that once the cream is skimmed from the unemployment pool, finding qualified trainees is going to become increasingly difficult.

Our industrialized society is comprised of a vast network of rapidly moving delicate and complex machines and scientific apparatus. It requires for its efficient and effective operation not only many educated and highly trained experts, but also a vast army of helpers who have an understanding of the relation of these machines and processes and who can read directions and carry out instructions. This requires a good command of the skills of communication—often referred to as functional literacy. Increased literacy is absolutely necessary to our expanding economy and technological growth. It will broaden the understanding, widen the horizon, and increase the flexibility of our workers. It will facilitate the adjustments and retraining made necessary by technological unemployment and by the lengthened period of retirement. It will open up new vistas and give new hope to that rapidly growing group of older persons in our population; and it will give impetus to the habit of life-long learning, thus helping to "keep the mind limber that tends to become inflexible with age."

Democracy, more than any other form of government, calls for a literate population. Our founding fathers recognized this; however, they did not specifically provide for its achievement in the organic law. Nevertheless, the principle has been so generally accepted that we have established the most comprehensive system of free universal compulsory education found anywhere in the world.

Despite this fact, we still have millions of adult Americans who suffer under the handicap of too little or no education; and this causes them to become a drag on society and a potential menace to our democratic way of life.

In order to function effectively in a democracy, citizens must possess facts about many things and people. If they are to exercise the kind of independent judgment which our representative form of government requires and are not to be unduly swayed by the rabble-rousers and the bombardment of mass media, they must think clearly and discriminatingly about those things and people. They cannot think clearly and independently unless they can participate effectively in the arts and skills of communication—which is functional literacy.

The individual is the cornerstone of our democracy, and to that extent is it necessary that there be a high rate of literacy among all groups of our population. Talk about "democracy" and "our way of life" is largely unintelligible to the large numbers of functional illiterates in our society.

Literacy Education Opportunities

Organization and administration. The problem of the elimination of illiteracy has many facets. Although the amount of functional illiteracy varies from state to state it occurs, in nearly all of them, in quantity sufficient to require a special program for its elimination. Only a very few states now have organized programs for the reduction of illiteracy. One of the major requirements in an adequate program would be an administrative and supervisory organization in the states which would have the authority and resources to plan and conduct literacy classes for the majority of adult illiterates who make up our large mass of undereducated Americans. Such an organization in each state, with the clear mission to do so, could reduce illiteracy to a minimum.

Teachers and supervisors. Effective instruction to develop adult literacy calls for trained, mature teachers who understand the interests and needs of adult illiterates and who can approach them with an understanding of adult psychology. The materials and methods for conducting literacy training need also to be adapted to the differing circumstances in various regions of the country. In the sparsely settled rural areas of the Southwest, for example, the methods of organizing literacy-training programs and the materials used in them need to be different from those developed for use in the industrial cities of the Northeast.

In order to provide essential services to teachers and supervisors in literacy-training programs, there should be at least five regional training and development centers. These centers should be staffed and equipped to furnish leadership in the training of teachers, supervisors, and other professional workers; to conduct research and demonstrations in the field of teaching methods; and to produce instructional materials.

Instructional materials. One of the major requirements in this task is the careful selection and development of suitable materials and methods for teaching adult illiterates. Efforts in this field often fail because materials and methods suitable for teaching children are offered to adults. Effective teaching will require new types of materials comparable to those prepared (1) for the Project for Adult Education of Negroes and (2) for the special training programs in the armed services during World War II.

In addition to the services of the five regional centers in developing and selecting suitable instructional materials, it would be necessary to provide consultative services and a clearinghouse of information on literacy education.

The complexity of the problems of illiteracy requires a comprehensive approach to their solution and the balanced effort of all government and private agencies directed toward helping members of this group help themselves. For more than a century, in a variety of ways, the Federal Government has provided aid to education in cooperation with the states and educational institutions. More recently, during and after World War II, it has enabled millions of service men and women to raise their levels of formal education while they were in the armed services and in educational programs for veterans . . . after their return to civilian life.

The increasing burden of education is already straining the financial capacity of many state and local governments. The role of the Federal Government therefore should be to stimulate, encourage, and reinforce local and state efforts to eliminate illiteracy. The recommendations which follow emphasize the types of action which will meet the most pressing and urgent needs, and lay a firm foundation against the needs of the future.

Present Provisions

It was estimated by the Office of Education in 1950 that fewer than 30,000 native-born adult illiterates were enrolled in public school literacy classes in the several states in 1949-50. In a survey of adult education activities of the public schools made by the Office of Education for 1947-48, out of the 2,684 school districts reporting, 351 had literacy education activities for adults. Although city school systems were serving more than rural systems, the limited provisions were widely distributed among forty-six states.

In school districts having a population of 50,000 or more, a slight majority, 51.4 per cent, offered literacy classes. In districts with populations of 10,000 to 50,000 it was 19 per cent; from 2,500 to 10,000, 4.7 per cent; 2,500 and less, 2.2 per cent; and in counties, 11.9 per cent. The study concluded:

Only one out of eight schools returning the checklist reported literacy education and one out of eight reported elementary education for adults. In 1947 an estimated 9,240,000 people, aged fourteen and above, had no more than four years of schooling and were classed as functionally illiterate. Obviously most public schools are doing very little or nothing to improve this situation.

Private and voluntary agencies have engaged in literacy teaching through the establishment of "opportunity schools," continuation or adult evening schools, and Americanization schools. In addition there was established, fairly recently, the National Commission for Adult Literacy.

Although pertinent, systematically gathered data are scant it seems reasonably certain that most of the literacy training thus far provided for adults has been so located and planned as to benefit immigrants rather than English-speaking native-born illiterates.

It is clear that few, if any, provisions exist for recruiting and training teachers or other specialists in literacy training, or for the development of functional materials for literacy-education programs. The dearth of literacy-training materials was dramatically emphasized in the experience of the army in World War II. Finding itself obliged to give basic elementary education to thousands of young soldiers, the army could find no materials suitable for the purpose and had to resort, in some instances, to hasty improvisation.

Underlying these practical provisions for the reduction of adult illiteracy are certain less direct and tangible facts which, nevertheless, exert a powerful influence.

One distressing fact is that adult illiteracy receives very little attention from the citizenry or from the educational profession. Although the Armed Forces have repeatedly called attention to it, and Federal officials have from time to time underscored its importance and expressed the hope that the matter would receive attention, the response has been meager. The causes of this neglect are readily apparent.

The country's educational agencies have been hard pressed to provide teachers and buildings for children and youth, so that little surplus of means or energy remain for other matters. Illiterate adults are ordinarily inarticulate and unorganized. This makes any effort to press their claims after the fashion of some other special interests increasingly difficult.

The time has arrived when we can no longer neglect to utilize the vast resources inherent in the large group of uneducated adults found in our population.

It is in the interest of their own individual well-being, as well as in the interest of the national welfare, that we cultivate the unused talents of these citizens. A majority of them have both the capacity and willingness to learn. We cannot achieve the goal of equality of opportunity to which our democracy subscribes so long as this group is forgotten educationally.

A crusade to wipe out the blot of illiteracy from our nation will have a salutary effect on our entire educational enterprise. It will not only give a tremendous impetus to our efforts to enforce our compulsory school attendance laws, but will also help to increase financial support of education. Such a crusade will improve our educational materials and methods generally, as well as provide millions with the tools of communication which are the means of developing more effective and fruitful citizens in all walks of life.

III. THE UNDERPRIVILEGED

EDITOR'S INTRODUCTION

Functional illiterates are not born; they are shaped by a host of economic and sociological factors. Today's undereducated adult may have had parents who were themselves illiterate and who scorned or disregarded the value of education. The undereducated adult may also have come from a home without books or pencils or papers. He may have lived in slum conditions, with too many people in too few rooms and where the environment was entirely unsuitable for study or reading. He may have attended overcrowded schools staffed by overworked teachers who had little time or opportunity to pay attention to individual differences and individual potentials. He may have been an indifferent student and have been eager to drop out of school. But whatever the specific factors that went into the making of an undereducated adult, it can usually be assumed that such a person was a member of some underprivileged group in our society.

While many of those in underprivileged groups have overcome the obstacles facing them, many others have been defeated by the challenge and some may not even have made much of an effort. The articles in this section have been chosen to stress the difficulties facing the underprivileged. The opening selection, written in connection with the Administration's antipoverty program, shows that the poor are often the undereducated and the undereducated are almost always the poor. The excerpt from John W. Gardner's book comments upon the stratification in our society and its impact on the young.

The article by Martin Deutsch illustrates in detail the disadvantages faced by a child from a culturally deprived background. The author explains, in rigorously technical language, just why there is likely to be a high proportion of school failures and dropouts in this group. Frank Riessman points out that the culturally deprived may often be slower learners, but states that there is no reason to equate this with stupidity or inability to learn. Dr. Riessman also maintains that there may well be gifted children among the slow learners and that efforts should be made by the schools to discover and encourage these students.

The remaining articles fill in the picture of the underprivileged in terms of their schooling. Warren Cutts writes of their unreadiness for reading and, presumably, for many of the other school activities that children from middle-class backgrounds handle with ease. Francis Keppel, United States Commissioner of Education, points out the danger of the "pass-along." This is the practice—often found in slum schools—of letting children pass from grade to grade even though they are not ready for advancement. By the eighth grade many of them may be two or more years behind in scholastic achievement and merely waiting for the first opportunity to drop out of school.

The articles in this section throw light on the great problems and challenges that face the country in this field. Some of them make suggestions for action. The programs that have already been put into operation and the proposals for further moves will be more fully explored in the last section of this compilation.

THE WAR ON POVERTY [1]

Patterns of poverty are established early in life. Thousands of children grow up in homes where education, ambition, and hope are as scarce as money. Many of these children attend school with little incentive or guidance from home to get them through. They drop out as soon at the law permits, or sooner. Others fail to attend school at all.

By the time such children reach sixteen, they begin a lifelong drift through a series of low-skill or no-skill jobs that grow increasingly harder to find as automation spreads through business

[1] From presentation prepared under the direction of R. Sargent Shriver, Jr., whom President Johnson selected in August 1964 to head the nation's antipoverty program. In *The War on Poverty: The Economic Opportunity Act of 1964;* a compilation of materials relevant to S. 2642 (the Economic Opportunity Act). United States. Senate. Committee on Labor and Public Welfare. 88th Congress, 2d session. Supt. of Docs. Washington, D.C. 20402. '64. p 36-45.

and industry. Some who can't find jobs at all turn to drug addiction, petty crime, then major crime.

But most simply find a niche of minimum usefulness to themselves and society, where they may cling for the rest of their lives. They need opportunities for escape, but first, their attitudes have to be rebuilt, in a sense, from the ground up. For poverty can be a state of mind, and many of these young people feel already defeated.

Another group falls in with this youthful army of the poor who form ranks in city slums and rural backwaters across the nation. These are children of poor families who grow up with the motivation and the ambition, but not the opportunities. If they get through high school they are unable to find part-time work to help them meet college expenses, or to help them contribute to needed support at home.

There are, in all, 11 million children among the 35 million poor of this nation. The leading edge of the postwar wave of infants has been reaching the critical sixteen-to-twenty-one age bracket for the past few years. There are 5.5 million in this bracket now. In a single month last fall, 730,000 of them were unemployed and not registered in schools. By 1970 there will be over 7 million in the sixteen-to-twenty-one group, and unless the trend is reversed the number of youths not working and not attending schools can be expected to total well over a million.

The Bypassed

Unparalleled technical advances in America have brought to most of our labor force and their families a standard of living undreamed of thirty years ago. But for a considerable minority it has brought considerably less.

There are thousands who are simply bypassed by modern technological advances. They are unable to secure regular employment in an economy which increasingly creates jobs beyond their meager skills and education.

There is also the semiskilled or unskilled worker, suddenly displaced from his job as the plant relocates, or as the machine takes over, who faces weeks or months of unemployment, or a forced retirement. Following a plant closing in Trenton in October 1961, 1,900 employees—almost two thirds of the work force—were still unemployed and looking for work nine months later. In Sioux City, Iowa, 40 per cent of the former employees remained unemployed six months after the June 1963 closing of their plant. In Iron City, Wisconsin, a mine closed in August of 1962, leaving about 40 per cent of the miners still looking for work nine months later. In Fargo, North Dakota, a third of the former employees were still unemployed a year after their plant closed.

Some of these workers, who have nontransferable skills or are "too old" at forty or fifty to be reabsorbed, are unable to get regular jobs or, in many cases, any work at all. They find themselves in a downward spiral that pulls their children down with them. Still others, somewhat luckier, are able to find steady work, but in low-pay occupations and industries, at wage rates which are insufficient to keep the family out of the grip of poverty.

Millions of workers inhabit this economic underworld of the bypassed.

The Rural Poor

Our technological upheaval has cast off another luckless group —the small farmer and the surrounding community which depends on his solvency. Some farmers have ridden the tides of our economic growth to unprecedented farm income levels. But many more, caught between falling agricultural prices and soaring investment costs, have found themselves in a trap that appears to offer no escape except perhaps to an unpromising new life in an urban slum.

One and a half million rural farm families live on less than $250 a month; 2.8 million other rural families in nonfarm occupations struggle along at the same income level. Over a million of these rural families must somehow stretch $80 a month to cover their needs. For the children of these families, without shoes or clothes for school, without money for school supplies or lunches, even primary education becomes a luxury. Nearly half a million of these rural youths between the ages of fourteen and twenty-four have completed no more than sixth grade. Their horizons thus stop at the edge of a few acres of exhausted land.

Nowhere is the irony of the poor being furnished with the poorest services more poignant than in the rural areas. Here are found the one-room schoolhouse held together by a single over-burdened teacher, the families too isolated to avail themselves of health services, the homesteads unable to apply the benefits of agricultural research.

Many rural farm families find that even a semibarren piece of land offers them more certitude than the prospect of a new life in a strange environment. With limited education or skills, or failing health, they have no choice but to squeeze some sustenance from the land they know.

Others have already joined the vanguard of an unhappy exodus, a growing legion of unskilled, uneducated workers who come to the city in search of something they may not find: better opportunities. Often they find they have accomplished nothing but a relocation of their poverty.

The Minority Poor

There is a substantial segment of the poor in this country who need not puzzle over the complicated economics of poverty. They are the minority group poor. For them the equations are simpler. They are hired last, paid less, and fired first. They work mainly in the low-pay occupations, and in those, get lower pay than their white counterparts. The Negro college graduate can expect to earn only as much income as the white worker who never went beyond the eighth grade; in comparable occupations, the white man can expect to earn almost 50 per cent more in his lifetime than the Negro and the Puerto Rican, almost one third more than the Spanish-speaking American.

Eight million Negroes—nearly half the total Negro population in the United States—are poor. A third of the Negro population lives in southern cities, one fourth on southern farms, and the balance largely in the northern cities. In both the North and the South the Negro faces the same problem: in relation to his white counterpart, he is falling further and further behind. During the fifties the average income of the Negro male improved substantially. For every dollar he earned in 1949, he earned $1.75 in 1959. But the white man running ahead of him ran a little faster. While the Negro was earning $1 in 1949, his white counterpart earned $1.90; in 1959, every time the Negro earned $1.75 the white man earned $3.20.

In twenty-four of the twenty-six states with large Negro populations, the Negro's share of per capita income fell; and in some of these states the gap between white and Negro income widened dramatically. In Michigan in 1949, when the equalizing effect of World War II was still being felt, the Negro earned 87 per cent as much as the white. Ten years later he earned only 75 per cent as much. In North Carolina his comparative earnings fell from 54 per cent of his white counterpart's to 43 per cent; in Tennessee, from 68 to 56 per cent; in Arkansas, from 53 to 39 per cent.

Nearly a million Puerto Ricans live in the United States today, primarily in metropolitan New York City. Fifty-three per cent of New York's Puerto Ricans earned less than $4,000 in 1959, only 8 per cent earned more than $8,000. Three quarters of them never entered high school. Moreover, the primary and junior high schools in Puerto Rican neighborhoods tend to be more crowded and less equipped than the average city school.

In the southwestern United States live 3.5 million Spanish-speaking Americans. Not only does the Spanish-American face the burdens of prejudice and inadequate education; like the Puerto Rican, he also faces a language barrier, and moreover a peculiar structure of laws, both Federal and local, which tend to isolate him even more from the opportunities of the community.

Among the poverty-stricken minorities, the American Indian is perhaps the hardest hit. Of the 550,000 American Indians, 380,000 live on or near reservations, most of them in poor circumstances. Their average family income is only a quarter to a third of the national average. Their average educational level is only half as high as the national average. And though they are American-born, go to American schools, and have received special attention from the Federal Government, social and economic barriers continue to pen them up in islands of poverty.

The Fatherless Families

Death, divorce, and disability often leave the same barren legacy. There are 2.3 million fatherless families in America who have inherited nothing but the father's poverty. Many of them were poor while the father was still present; some are poor because the father is disabled, or deserted or died; and some are fatherless because they are poor. Low-income families often live with far more strains—financial, physical, and moral—than comfortable families, and these strains may reach the point where the father unshoulders his burden by deserting.

With a crushing responsibility suddenly thrust upon her, the mother is often too ill equipped to carry it. Frequently the presence of young children forces her to remain at home. Even if adequate day care arrangements can be made, or if the children are older, the mother may lack education, training, or experience needed to get an adequate job.

Only 16 per cent of the mothers of families receiving public assistance have completed high school; less than 10 per cent have had experience in office or sales work or in related occupations, as against 40 per cent of mothers not on welfare. Most of these mothers of fatherless families have had experience chiefly as domestics, service workers, and unskilled laborers.

The likelihood that such mothers will find employment which will furnish the stability and income so sorely neded in the absence of an able, breadwinning father up to now has been remote. Only half the fatherless families in the nation are above the poverty line. . . .

Youth—Salvaging a Vital Resource

In October of 1963, there were 730,000 young men and women between the ages of sixteen and twenty-one who were both out of school and out of work. This figure had increased 22 per cent in a one-year period. But this unemployment figure for a specific week in October does not tell the whole story. Many others are employed only in low-paying, dead-end jobs which are beneath their potential abilities. A conservative estimate is that there are almost 1 million young people in this country today who are desperately in need of training and guidance to develop these abilities. Left to itself, the problem will multiply. Last year the total teen-age labor force, including half a million young people in the Armed Forces, numbered 5.6 million. Next year it will be 6.6 million. By 1970, it will be 7.2 million. If the current trends continue, in five years we will have almost 1.5 million unemployed youth—without adequate education or training, without jobs, and without a future.

This trend must be reversed. And it can be reversed, by attacking the tight circle of poverty at its weakest point—among its young victims, whose creative energies and dreams may still be salvaged from the growing rubble of their lives.

The proposed legislation [enacted into law in August 1964] includes three different programs aimed at the attitudes and economics of the young. The first of these is a voluntary Job Corps, with camp-based programs of education and vocational training or conservation work for young men who are poorly adjusted to their homes and work. These young men cannot be helped best in programs located within their own communities. Some are in the migrant labor stream—at home nowhere. Others are outside the range of communities where adequate resources and concern exist. Still others come from impoverished rural areas and remote mountain hollows, or from city slums which have taught them only hostility to their environment. These young people must come a long way; the spark of motivation is not likely to be ignited in the same communities which have so long stifled it.

The education program in conservation camps will be designed to meet the needs of young men who are so lacking in basic academic skills that they cannot undertake vocational training. (A fifth- to sixth-grade literacy equivalency is considered necessary to profit from vocational training. An analysis of Selective Service System rejectees indicates that over half of those who fail to meet mental achievement requirements will be below this level.) Reading, writing, arithmetic, and speech will be taught, and minimum levels to be obtained are as follows:

Reading. An ability to read and comprehend at mean seventh-grade level.

Writing. An ability to complete, clearly and legibly, application and other employment forms, to write simple letters of inquiry, and to make out orders.

Arithmetic. An understanding and mastery of the four basic skills (addition, subtraction, multiplication, and division), common and decimal fractions, reading of scales, units of measurement.

Speaking. An ability to be understood in employment and other conventional situations, and to understand directions.

To reach these goals, new instructional materials designed especially for the purpose will be developed. But the education component of the program cannot wait. The availability of current materials will be reviewed by the Office of Education, and those determined to be best suited will be used. Continuing evaluation of the camps' programs will provide guidance for the development of new materials.

Group discussions, films, individual counseling, and specially selected readings will be used to instill in the young men an understanding of their role as citizens and workers. The same techniques will be used to teach the fundamentals of personal health and hygiene.

Camp recreation will include hobbies and sports, designed to teach the value of learning to play by the rules and to exercise self-discipline. The emphasis will be placed on participation rather than on observance. In addition, specific all-camp activities will be held on a regular basis; singing, a camp newspaper, and amateur dramatics will be used to promote the over-all purpose of the program; and a system of recognition and awards for achievement will be created.

Other aspects of camp life will also be designed to improve the attitudes of the young men involved. A typical camp might have some five to ten cabins of twenty young men each, with one adult resident and two youth assistants in every cabin. This responsibility will be rotated regularly, so that each may have a chance to lead. In addition, each cabin group will elect one representative to a camp council, designed to instill an appreciation of democratic principles.

The unifying force in the life of the camp will be a counseling program, dealing with every aspect of the experience—living, work, education, and recreation. At the end of each young man's tour, the counselors will have the major responsibility for guiding him to placement opportunities or further vocational training through the United States Employment Service.

VESTIGES OF STRATIFICATION [2]

One of the obstacles to the full development of talent in our society is that we still have not achieved full equality of opportunity.

In stratified societies, the amount of education received by a child depended upon his status in the society. If he was born to rank and wealth he had access to a good education. If he was born in the lower strata he usually did not. In this way, the educational system confirmed and held in place differences in status which were hereditarily determined. . . .

The history of American education has been one long campaign to get as far away from that kind of system as effort and ingenuity could take us. "Geniuses will be raked from the rubbish . . ." wrote Thomas Jefferson. But despite the efforts of generations of Americans to nullify the principles of stratification in our educational system, it still has a good deal of vitality. Most of the obvious positive steps toward true equality of opportunity have been taken; yet major inequalities of opportunity

[2] From *Excellence—Can We be Equal and Excellent Too?* by John W. Gardner, president of the Carnegie Corporation of New York and the Carnegie Foundation for the Advancement of Teaching. Harper & Row. New York. '61. p 38-41. Copyright © 1961 by John W. Gardner. Reprinted with the permission of Harper & Row, Publishers, Incorporated.

stemming from birth remain. And it will be a formidable task to eradicate these. Being born a Negro, for example, involves obvious limitations on educational opportunity in some parts of the country, and less obvious limitations in *all* parts of the country.

Despite our system of free schools, poverty can still be a profound handicap and wealth a clear advantage. The families at the lowest economic level must all too often live in a slum or near-slum area where the schools do not attract the best teachers. The prosperous citizen can afford a house in an expensive suburb which has a fine school. The good suburban schools are sociologically not unlike the good independent prep schools. The chief difference is that in the suburb, establishing residence is a part— and a very expensive part—of the price of admission (the other part being heavy school taxes). In a way the private prep school is more democratic because it takes in a number of scholarship students of truly impoverished parents. There is no possibility of such an arrangement in Scarsdale [a wealthy suburban community near New York City]. A youngster cannot attend the Scarsdale schools unless his parents live in Scarsdale; and that is something that impoverished parents do not commonly do.

Some of the problems associated with poverty are well illustrated in a case which was brought to my attention several years ago. When Tom B. was a senior in high school, the principal told him his grades were high enough to get him to a good college. Tom took a job in an aircraft factory instead. The principal couldn't understand it, but most of Tom's family and friends would not have understood any other decision. Tom's father, an invalid whose own education ended with the fourth grade, was genuinely—if profanely—proud of Tom's attainments ("The kid already talks like a —— dictionary!"), but thought the boy was already overeducated. His mother, a clerk in the five-and-ten, liked the idea of his going to college but needed his help to support the family. The wages offered by the factory looked like a fortune to Tom. He had worked part time since he was eight, but this was a man's job for a man's pay. He took it.

Actually, poverty is usually accompanied by other complicating factors, and this was so in Tom's case. If he had had a fierce determination to go on to college, he might have found a way. But his diet was deficient in other things besides money. There were virtually no books in Tom's home. No one ever talked about ideas. No one ever mentioned educational goals. Most of Tom's pals in the run-down part of town where he lived had quit school long since. He had literally never had an informal out-of-school chat with anyone who reminisced about his own college years or recommended college to him. It is not surprising, then, that he had no awareness of what college could mean, no motivation to use his fine mind, no aspirations that involved intellectual performance. The image of a fat pay check from the aircraft company was very real; and the image of college was very pale.

Only in recent years have we come to the realization that these deficiencies are as damaging as any monetary handicap. The son of the city's leading lawyer had financial resources that Tom did not have; but even more important, he had an awareness of intellectual values and educational goals. This awareness was passed on to him as a hereditary advantage—in much the same way that money and a title of nobility are passed on. . . .

Differences in educational opportunity will never be completely eradicated, but they must be reduced in scope and significance. Americans rightly resent the disparities of social background and the prejudices which limit the recognition of talent wherever it occurs. They will continue to do so as long as such disparities and prejudices exist.

But it would be wrong to leave the impression that stratification of educational opportunity is still a dominant feature of our sysem. It is not. The vestiges of stratification still exist, but the great drama of American education has been the democratization of educational opportunity over the past century. This has been one of the great social revolutions. In emphasizing that much ground remains to be won, we must not belittle the victories already achieved.

THE DISADVANTAGED CHILD AND THE LEARNING PROCESS [3]

Among children who come from lower-class socially impoverished circumstances, there is a high proportion of school failure, school dropouts, reading and learning disabilities, as well as life adjustment problems. This means not only that these children grow up poorly equipped academically, but also that the effectiveness of the school as a major institution for socialization is diminished. The effect of this process is underlined by the fact that this same segment of the population contributes disproportionately to the delinquency and other social deviancy statistics.

The thesis here is that the lower-class child enters the school situation so poorly prepared to produce what the school demands that initial failures are almost inevitable, and the school experience becomes negatively rather than positively reinforced. Thus the child's experience in school does nothing to counteract the invidious influences to which he is exposed in his slum, and sometimes segregated, neighborhood.

We know that children from underprivileged environments tend to come to school with a qualitatively different preparation for the demands of both the learning process and the behavioral requirements of the classroom. These are various differences in the kinds of socializing experiences these children have had, as contrasted with the middle-class child. The culture of their environment is a different one from the culture that has molded the school and its educational techniques and theory.

We know that it is difficult for all peoples to span cultural discontinuities, and yet we make little if any effort to prepare administrative personnel or teachers and guidance staff to assist the child in this transition from one cultural context to another. This transition must have serious psychological consequences for the child, and probably plays a major role in influencing his later perceptions of other social institutions as he is introduced to them. . . .

[3] From article by Martin P. Deutsch, associate professor of psychiatry and director of the Institute for Development Studies, New York Medical College. From *Education in Depressed Areas*, edited by A. Harry Passow. p 163-75. Copyright © 1963 by Teachers College, Columbia University. Reprinted by permission of the Bureau of Publications, Teachers College, Columbia University. All rights reserved.

Environmental Factors

While it is likely that slum life might have delimited areas that allow for positive growth and that the middle-class community has attributes which might retard healthy development, generally the combination of circumstances in middle-class life is considerably more likely to furnish opportunities for normal growth of the child. At the same time, slum conditions are more likely to have deleterious effects on physical and mental development. This is not to say that middle-class life furnishes a really adequate milieu for the maximum development of individual potential: it doesn't. The fact that we often speak as though it does is a function of viewing the middle-class environment in comparison to the slum. Middle-class people who work and teach across social-class lines often are unable to be aware of the negative aspects of the middle-class background because of its apparent superiority over the less advantageous background provided by lower-class life. We really have no external criterion for evaluating the characteristics of a millieu in terms of how well it is designed to foster development; as a result we might actually be measuring one area of social failure with the yardstick of social catastrophe.

It is true that many leading personalities in twentieth century American life have come from the slums, and this is a fact often pointed out . . . in an effort to prove that if the individual "has it in him" he can overcome—and even be challenged by—his humble surroundings. This argument, though fundamentally fallacious, might have had more to recommend it in the past. At the turn of the century we were a massively vertical mobile society—that is, with the exception of certain large minority groups such as the Negroes, the Indians, and the Mexican-Americans who were rarely allowed on the social elevator. In the mid-twentieth century, it is now increasingly possible for all groups to get on, but social and economic conditions have changed, and the same elevator more frequently moves in two directions or stands still altogether. When it does move, it goes more slowly, and, most discouragingly, it also provides an observation window on what, at least superficially, appears to be a most affluent society. Television, movies, and other media continually expose the individual from the slum to the explicit assumption that the products of a consumer society are available to all—or, rather, as he sees it, to all but him. In effect, this means that the child from the disadvantaged environment is an outsider and an observer—through his own eyes and those of his parents or neighbors—of the mainstream of American life. At the same time, when the child enters school he is exposing himself directly to the values and anticipations of a participant in that mainstream —his teacher. It is not sufficiently recognized that there is quite a gap between the training of a teacher and the needs, limitations, and unique strengths of the child from a marginal situation. This gap is, of course, maximized when the child belongs to a minority group that until quite recently was not only excluded from the mainstream, but was not even allowed to bathe in the tributaries.

What are some of the special characteristics of these children, and why do they apparently need exceptional social and educational planning? So often, administrators and teachers say, they are children who are "curious," "cute," "affectionate," "warm," and independently dependent in the kindergarten and the first grade, but who so often become "alienated," "withdrawn," "angry," "passive," "apathetic," or just "troublemakers" by the fifth and sixth grade. . . . It is in the first grade that we usually see the smallest differences between socioeconomic or racial groups in intellectual, language, and some conceptual measures, and in the later grades that we find the greatest differences in favor of the more socially privileged groups. From both teachers' observations and the finding of this increasing gap, it appears that there is a failure on some level of society and, more specifically, the educational system. Was the school scientifically prepared to receive these children in the first place? And, in addition, were the children perhaps introduced to the individual demands of the larger culture at too late an age—that is, in first grade?

Before discussing these psychological products of social deprivation, it is appropriate to look more closely at the special circumstances of Negro slum residents. In the core city of most of our large metropolitan areas, 40 to 70 per cent of the elementary school population is likely to be Negro. In my observations, through workshops in many of these cities, I have often been surprised to find how little real comprehension of the particular problems of these youngsters exists as part of the consciousness of the Negro or white middle-class teachers. While in middle-class schools there is great sensitivity to emotional climates and pressures and tensions that might be operating on the child in either the home or the school, in lower-class schools the problems of social adaptation are so massive that sensitivity tends to become blunted.

In the lower-class Negro group there still exists the . . . [consequences] of the conditions of slavery. While a hundred years have passed, this is a short time in the life of a people. And the extension of tendrils of the effects of slavery into modern life has been effectively discouraged only in the last few decades, when there have been some real attempts to integrate the Negro fully into American life. It is often difficult for teachers and the personnel of other community agencies to understand the Negro lower-class child—particularly the child who has come, or whose parents have come, from the rural South. There is a whole set of implicit and explicit value systems which determine our educational philosophies, and the institutional expectation is that all children participate in these systems. And yet for these expectations to be met, the child must experience some continuity of sociocultural participation in and sharing of these value systems before he comes to school. This is often just not the case for the child who comes from an encapsulated community, particularly when the walls have been built by the dominant social and cultural forces that have also determined the value systems relating to learning.

A recent article in *Fortune* magazine asked why the Negro failed to take full advantage of opportunities open to him in

American life. At least part of the answer is that the Negro has not been fully integrated into American life, and that even knowledge about particular occupations and their requirements is not available outside the cultural mainstream. . . .

Another source of misunderstanding on the part of school and social agency people is the difficulty of putting in historical perspective the causal conditions responsible for the high percentage of broken homes in the Negro community. Implications of this for the child's emotional stability are very frequently recognized, but the effects on the child's motivation, self-concept, and achievement orientation are not often understood.

The Negro family was first broken deliberately by the slave traders and the plantation owners for their own purposes. As was pointed out earlier, the hundred years since slavery is not a very long time for a total social metamorphosis even under fostering conditions—and during that period the Negro community has been for the most part economically marginal and isolated from the contacts which would have accelerated change. The thirteen depressions and recessions we have had since Emancipation have been devastating to this community. These . . . social circumstances have been particularly harsh on the Negro male. The chronic instability has greatly influenced the Negro man's concept of himself and his general motivation to succeed in competitive areas of society where the rewards are greatest. All these circumstances have contributed to the instability of the Negro family, and particularly to the fact that it is most often broken by the absence of the father. As a result, the lower-class Negro child entering school often has had no experience with a "successful" male model or thereby with a psychological framework in which effort can result in at least the possibility of achievement. Yet the value system of the school and of the learning process is predicated on the assumption that effort will result in achievement.

To a large extent, much of this is true not only for the Negro child but for all children who come from impoverished and marginal social and economic conditions. These living conditions are characterized by great overcrowding in substandard housing, often lacking adequate sanitary and other facilities. While we don't know the actual importance, for example, of moments of privacy, we do know that the opportunity frequently does not exist. In addition, there are likely to be large numbers of siblings and half-siblings, again with there being little opportunity for individuation. At the same time, the child tends to be restricted to his immediate environment, with conducted explorations of the "outside" world being infrequent and sometimes nonexistent. In the slums, and to an unfortunately large extent in many other areas of our largest cities, there is little opportunity to observe natural beauty, clean landscapes or other pleasant and aesthetically pleasing surroundings.

In the child's home, there is a scarcity of objects of all types, but especially of books, toys, puzzles, pencils, and scribbling paper. It is not that the mere presence of such materials would necessarily result in their productive use, but it would increase the child's familiarity with the tools he'll be confronted with in school. Actually, for the most effective utilization of these tools, guidance and explanations are necessary from the earliest time of exposure. Such guidance requires not only the presence of aware and educated adults, but also time—a rare commodity in these marginal circumstances. Though many parents will share in the larger value system of having high aspirations for their children, they are unaware of the operational steps required for the preparation of the child to use optimally the learning opportunities in the school. Individual potential is one of the most unmarketable properties if the child acquires no means for its development, or if no means exist for measuring it objectively. It is here that we must understand the consequences of all these aspects of the slum matrix for the psychological and cognitive development of the child. . . .

In individual terms, a child is probably farther away from his maturational ceiling as a result of this experiential poverty. This might well be a crucial factor in the poorer performance of the lower socioeconomic children on standardized tests of intelligence. . . .

This suggests a limitation on the frequent studies comparing Negro and white children. Even when it is possible to control for the formal attributes of social class membership, the uniqueness of the Negro child's experience would make comparability impossible when limited to these class factors. Perhaps too, if such an interaction exists between experiential and biological determinants of development, it would account for the failure of the culture-free tests, as they too are standardized on an age basis without allowing for the experiential interaction (as distinguished from specific experiential *influence*).

Let us now consider some of the specifics in the child's environment, and their effects on the development of the formal, contentual, and attitudinal systems.

Visually, the urban slum and its overcrowded apartments offer the child a minimal range of stimuli. There are usually few if any pictures on the wall, and the objects in the household, be they toys, furniture, or utensils, tend to be sparse, repetitious, and lacking in form and color variations. The sparsity of objects and lack of diversity of home artifacts which are available and meaningful to the child, in addition to the unavailability of individualized training, gives the child few opportunities to manipulate and organize the visual properties of his environment and thus perceptually to organize and discriminate the nuances of that environment. These would include figure-ground relationships and the spatial organization of the visual field. The sparsity of manipulable objects probably also hampers the development of these functions in the tactile area. For example, while these children have broomsticks and usually a ball, possibly a doll or a discarded kitchen pot to play with, they don't have the different shapes and colors and sizes to manipulate which the middle-class child has in the form of blocks which are bought just for him, or even in the variety of sizes and shapes of cooking utensils which might be available to him as playthings.

It is true, as has been pointed out frequently, that the pioneer child didn't have many playthings either. But he had a more active responsibility toward the environment and a great variety of growing plants and other natural resources as well as a stable family that assumed a primary role for the education and training of the child. In addition, the intellectually normal or superior frontier child could and usually did grow up to be a farmer. Today's child will grow up into a world of automation requiring highly differentiated skills if he and society are to use his intellect.

The effect of sparsity of manipulable objects on visual perception is, of course, quite speculative, as few data now exist. However, it is an important area, as among skills necessary for reading are form discrimination and visual spatial organization. Children from depressed areas, because of inadequate training and stimulation, may not have developed the requisite skills by the time they enter first grade, and the assumption that they do possess these skills may thus add to the frustration these children experience on entering school.

The lower-class home is not a verbally oriented environment. . . . Let us consider . . . [the] implication for the development of auditory discrimination skills. While the environment is a noisy one, the noise is not, for the most part, meaningful in relation to the child, and for him most of it is background. In the crowded apartments with all the daily living stresses, is a minimum of noninstructional conversation directed toward the child. In actuality, the situation is ideal for the child to learn inattention. Furthermore, he does not get practice in auditory discrimination or feedback from adults correcting his enunciation, pronunciation, and grammar. In studies at the Institute for Developmental Studies at New York Medical College . . . we have found significant differences in auditory discrimination between lower-class and middle-class children in the first grade. These differences seem to diminish markedly as the children get older, though the effects of their early existence on other functioning remain to be investigated. Here again, we are dealing with a skill very important to reading. Our data indicate too that poor readers within social-class groups have significantly more difficulty in auditory discrimination than do good readers. Further, the difference between good and poor readers is greater for the lower-class group.

If the child learns to be inattentive in the preschool environment, as has been postulated, this further diminishes incoming stimulation. Further, if this trained inattention comes about as a result of his being insufficiently called upon to respond to particular stimuli, then his general level of responsiveness will also be diminished. The nature of the total environment and the child-adult interaction is such that reinforcement is too infrequent, and, as a result, the quantity of response is diminished. The implications of this for the structured learning situation in the school are quite obvious.

Related to attentivity is memory. Here also we would postulate the dependence of the child, particularly in the preschool period, on interaction with the parent. It is adults who link the past and the present by calling to mind prior shared experiences. The combination of the constriction in the use of language and in shared activity results, for the lower-class child, in much less stimulation of the early memory function. Although I don't know of any data supporting this thesis, from my observations it would seem that there is a tendency for these children to be proportionately more present-oriented and less aware of past-present sequences than the middle-class child. . . . While this could be a function of the poorer time orientation of these children or of their difficulty in verbal expression, . . . it could also relate to a greater difficulty in seeing themselves in the past or in a different context. Another area which points up the home-school discontinuity is that of time. Anthropologists have pointed out that from culture to culture time concepts differ and that time as life's governor is a relatively modern phenomenon and one which finds most of its slaves in the lower-middle, middle-middle, and upper-middle classes. It might not even be an important factor in learning, but it is an essential feature in the measurement of children's performance by testing and in the adjustment of children to the organizational demands of the school. The middle-class teacher organizes the day by allowing a certain amount of time for each activity. Psychologists have long noticed that American Indian children, mountain children, and children from other nonindustrial groups have great difficulty organizing their response tempo to meet time limitations. In the Orientation Scale developed at the Institute, we have found that lower-class children in the first grade had significantly greater difficulty than did middle-class children in handling items related to time judgments.

Another area in which the lower-class child lacks preschool orientation is the well-inculcated expectation of reward for performance, especially for successful task completion. The lack of such expectation, of course, reduces motivation for beginning a task and, therefore, also makes less likely the self-reinforcement of activity through the gaining of feelings of competence. In these impoverished, broken homes there is very little of the type of interaction seen so commonly in middle-class homes, in which the parent sets a task for the child, observes its performance, and in some way rewards its completion. Neither, for most tasks, is there the disapproval which the middle-class child incurs when he does not perform properly or when he leaves something unfinished. Again, much of the organization of the classroom is based on the assumption that children anticipate rewards for performance and that they will respond in these terms to tasks which are set for them. This is not to imply that the young lower-class child is not given assignments in his home, nor that he is never given approval or punishment. Rather, the assignments tend to be motoric in character, have a short time-span, and are more likely to relate to very concrete objects or services for people. The tasks given to preschool children in the middle class are more likely to involve language and conceptual processes, and are thereby more attuned to the later school setting.

Related to the whole issue of the adult-child dynamic in establishing a basis for the later learning process is the ability of the child to use the adult as a source for information, correction and the reality testing involved in problem solving and the absorption of new knowledge. When free adult time is greatly limited, homes vastly overcrowded, economic stress chronic, and the general educational level very low—and, in addition, when adults in our media culture are aware of the inadequacy of their education—questions from children are not encouraged, as the adults might be embarrassed by their own limitations and anyway are too preoccupied with the business of just living and surviving. In the child's formulation of concepts of the world, the ability to formulate questions is an essential step in data gathering. If questions are not encouraged or if they are not responded to, this is a function which does not mature. . . .

In our observation of children at the kindergarten level and in our discussions with parents, we find that many lower-class children have difficulty here. It follows that this problem, if it is not compensated for by special school efforts, becomes more serious later in the learning process, as more complex subject matter is introduced. It is here that questioning is not only desirable but essential, for if the child is not prepared to demand clarification he again falls farther behind, the process of alienation from school is facilitated, and his inattentiveness becomes further reinforced as he just does not understand what is being presented.

It is generally agreed that the language-symbolic process plays an important role at all levels of learning. . . . There are various dimensions of language, and for each of these it is possible to evaluate the influence of the verbal environment of the home and its immediate neighborhood.

In order for a child to handle multiple attributes of words and to associate words with their proper referents, a great deal of exposure to language is presupposed. Such exposure involves training, experiencing with identifying objects and having corrective feedback, listening to a variety of verbal material, and just observing adult language usage. Exposure of children to this type of experience is one of the great strengths of the middle-class home, and concomitantly represents a weakness in the lower-class home. In a middle-class home also, the availability of a great range of objects to be labeled and verbally related to each other strengthens the over-all language fluency of the child and gives him a basis for both understanding the teacher and for being able to communicate with her on various levels. An implicit hypothesis in a recent . . . survey of verbal skills is that verbal fluency is strongly related to reading skills and to other highly organized integrative and conceptual verbal activity.

The acquisition of language facility and fluency and experience with the multiple attributes of words is particularly important in view of the estimate that only 60 to 80 per cent of any sustained communication is usually heard. Knowledge of context and of the syntactical regularities of a language make correct completion and comprehension of the speech sequence possible. This completion occurs as a result of the correct anticipation of the sequence of language and thought. The child who has not achieved these anticipatory language skills is greatly handicapped in school. Thus for the child who already is deficient in auditory discrimination and in ability to sustain attention, it becomes increasingly important that he have the very skills he lacks most.

The problem in developing preventive and early remedial programs for these children is in determining the emphasis on the various areas that need remediation. For example, would it be more effective to place the greatest emphasis on the training of auditory discrimination, or on attentional mechanisms, or on anticipatory receptive language functions in order to achieve the primary goal of enabling the child to understand his teacher? In programing special remedial procedures, we do not know how much variation we will find from child to child, or if social-class experiences create a sufficiently homogeneous pattern of deficit so that the fact of any intervention and systematic training may be more important than its sequences. It this is so, the intervention would probably be most valid in the language area, because the large group of lower-class children with the kinds of deficits mentioned are probably . . . ready for more complex language functioning than they have achieved. Language knowledge, once acquired, can be self-reinforcing in just communicating with peers or talking to oneself.

In observations of lower-class homes, it appears that speech sequences seem to be temporally very limited and poorly structured syntactically. It is thus not surprising to find that a major focus of deficit in the children's language development is syntactical organization and subject continuity. In preliminary analysis of exposure and receptive language data on samples of middle- and lower-class children at the first- and fifth-grade levels, there are indications that the lower-class child has more expressive language ability than is generally recognized or than emerges in the classroom. The main differences between the social classes seem to lie in the level of syntactical organization. If, as is indicated in this research, with proper stimulation a surprisingly high level of expressive language functioning is available to the same children who show syntactical deficits, then we might conclude that the language variables we are dealing with here are by-products of social experience rather than indices of basic ability or intellectual level. This again suggests another possibly vital area to be included in an enrichment or a remedial program: training in the use of word sequences to relate and unify cognitions.

Also on the basis of preliminary analysis of data, it appears that retarded readers have the most difficulty with the organization of expressive language.

In another type of social-class-related language analysis, Bernstein, an English sociologist, has pointed out that the lower class tends to use informal language and mainly to convey concrete needs and immediate consequences, while the middle-class usage tends to be more formal and to emphasize the relating of concepts. This difference between these two milieus, then, might explain the finding in some of our recent research that the middle-class fifth-grade child has an advantage over the lower-class fifth grader in tasks where precise and somewhat abstract language is required for solution. Further, Bernstein's reasoning would again emphasize the communication gap which exists between the middle-class teacher and the lower-lass child.

Though it might belong more in the formal than in the contentual area, one can postulate that the absence of well-structured routine and activity in the home is reflected in the difficulty that the lower-class child has in structuring language. The implication of this for curriculum in the kindergarten and nursery school would be that these children should be offered a great deal of verbalized routine and regulation so that expectation can be built up in the child and then met.

THE CULTURALLY DEPRIVED CHILD: A NEW VIEW [4]

Most disadvantaged children are relatively slow in performing intellectual tasks. This slowness is an important feature of their mental style, and it needs to be carefully evaluated. In considering the question of slowness, we could do well to recognize that we probably put far too much emphasis on speed. We reward speed. We think of the fast child as the smart child and the slow child as the dull child. I think this is a false idea. I think there is much weakness in speed and much strength in slowness.

The teacher can be motivated to develop techniques for rewarding slow pupils if she understands the positive attributes of a slow style of learning. She should know that a pupil may be slow because he is extremely careful, meticulous, or cautious; because he usually refuses to generalize; or because he cannot understand an idea unless he does something physically—for example, with his hands—in connection with the idea he is trying to grasp. The disadvantaged child is typically a physical learner, and the physical learner is generally a slow learner. . . .

A child may be slow because he learns in a one-track way; that is, he persists in one line of thought and is not flexible or broad. He does not easily shift from one frame of reference to another, and consequently may appear slow and dull.

Analysis of the many reasons for slowness indicates that it should not be equated with stupidity. In fact there is no reason

[4] From article by Dr. Frank Riessman, Department of Psychiatry, Albert Einstein College of Medicine, New York City, formerly consultant for Mobilization for Youth, an organization dedicated to helping the undereducated. *School Life.* 45:5-7. Ap. '63.

to assume that there are not many slow gifted children. We must begin to search for excellence among the slow learners as well as among the fast. . . .

The assumption that the slow pupil is not bright functions as a self-fulfilling prophecy. If teachers act toward pupils as if they were dull, many pupils will come to function in this way. The average person, even in college, needs reinforcement. The teacher must pick up what he says, appeal to him, and pitch examples to him. The typical teacher does not do these things with a slow child. In my own teaching I easily fall into the habit of rewarding pupils whose faces light up when I talk, who are quick to respond to me, and I respond back to them. I remember what they say and use it in examples. I do not pick up the slow pupil, and I do not respond to him. He has to make it on his own. In the teacher training programs future teachers should be taught to guard against the almost unconscious and automatic tendency to respond to the pupil who responds to him.

Hidden Verbal Ability

Everybody in the school system has heard, at one time or other, that disadvantaged children have a verbal deficit, that they are inarticulate, nonverbal. But isn't this too simple a generalization? Aren't these children quite verbal out of school? That they can be highly articulate in conversation with their friends is illustrated by the language developed by urban Negro groups, some of which has been absorbed into the main culture.

Many questions about the verbal potential of disadvantaged children must be answered by research. Under what conditions are they verbal? What kind of stimuli do they respond to verbally? With whom are they verbal? What do they talk about? What parts of speech do they use? . . .

Disadvantaged children are often surprisingly articulate in role playing. One day I asked a group of such youngsters, "Why are you sore at the teachers?" Even though I was on good terms with them, I couldn't get much of a response. However, when I held a role-playing session in which some of them acted out the part of teachers and others the part of pupils, these "inarticulate" youngsters changed sharply. Within a half-hour they were bubbling over with verbal and sensitive answers to the question I had asked. They were telling me about the expressions on teachers' faces that they didn't like. They reported that they knew the minute they entered the room that the teacher didn't like them and that she didn't think they were going to do well in school. Their analyses were specific and remarkably verbal.

But the quality of their language has its limitations, and herein, I think, lies the deficit. . . . The difference is between formal language and public language, between the language of a written book and the informal everyday language. There is no question in my mind that disadvantaged children are deficient in formal language.

Since the deficit is clear, we might ask, "Why make such an issue of the positive verbal ability of these children?" The reason is that it is easy to believe, and too many people have come to believe, that this deficit in formal language means that deprived people are *characteristically* nonverbal.

If the schools accept the idea that these pupils are basically very good verbally, teachers might approach them in a different manner. Teachers might look for additional techniques to bring out their verbal ability; instead of predicting that they would not go very far in school, they might predict that they would go very far because they have good verbal ability. In other words, an awareness of the positive verbal ability (not merely potential) might lead them to demand more of the disadvantaged child and expect more of him.

Education Versus the School

There is a great deal of evidence that deprived children and their parents have a much more positive attitude toward education than is generally believed. This attitude is often obscured by the fact that deprived persons value education but dislike school. They are alienated from the school, and they resent the teachers. For the sake of clarity, we should consider their attitudes toward education and toward the school separately.

A nation-wide survey conducted by Elmo Roper after World War II asked, "If you had a son or daughter graduating from high school, would you prefer to have him or her go on to college? Do something else? Wouldn't care?" About 68 per cent of the poor and 91 per cent of the more prosperous chose college. The difference is significant, but 68 per cent is still a large figure and it indicates that a large number of poorer people are interested in a college education for their children.

Why do these people who have a positive attitude toward education have a negative attitude toward the school? These youngsters and their parents recognize that they are second-class citizens in the school, and they are angry about it. From the classroom to the PTA they discover that the school does not like them, does not respond to them, does not appreciate their culture, and does not think they can learn.

These children and their parents do not easily accept such reasons for education as "developing yourself," "expressing yourself," "gaining knowledge for its own sake." They want education much more for vocational reasons. Even so, they have a positive attitude toward education, particularly the lower socioeconomic Negro groups. In the Higher Horizons program in New York City [see "Higher Horizons," in Section IV, below] the parents have participated eagerly once they have seen that the school system is concerned about their children. One of the positive features of this program . . . [is its] concern for disadvantaged children. This the disadvantaged have not experienced before; and I believe that even if the programs did nothing else, the parents and children would be responsive and would become involved in the school because of this concern.

Some Weaknesses

A basic weakness of deprived youngsters which the school can deal with is the lack of know-how, including the academic know-how and the know-how of the middle class generally—knowing how to get a job, how to appear for an interview, how to fill out a form, how to take tests, how to answer questions, and how to listen. The last is particularly important. The whole style of learning of the deprived is not set to respond to oral or written stimuli. These children respond more readily to visual and kinesthetic signals. We should remodel the school to suit the styles and meet their needs. But no matter how much we change the school to suit their needs, we have to change these children in some ways—in reading, formal language, test-taking, and general know-how.

These weaknesses represent deficiencies in skills and techniques. There is only one value of the lower socioeconomic groups which I would fight in the school—their anti-intellectual attitude. I am very much opposed to spending a lot of time in teaching values to these youngsters. I am much concerned, and in this I am traditional, that the schools impart skills, techniques, and knowledge to them instead of training them to become good middle-class children.

I believe, however, that the attitude of these youngsters toward intellectuals, toward knowledge for its own sake, and similar issues has to be fought out in the schools. These children and their parents are pretty much anti-intellectual at all levels. They don't like "eggheads"; they think talk is "a lot of bull." I would consciously oppose this attitude in the school. I would make the issue explicit; there would be nothing subtle or covert about it. I would state clearly that the school does not agree with them on this point and is prepared to argue about the views they hold.

Summary and Implications

I have attempted to reinterpret some of the supposedly negative aspects that characterize the cognitive style of disadvantaged persons and to call attention to their untapped verbal ability. But there are other positive features of the culture and style of the deprived . . . : The cooperativeness that marks the large family; the informality and humor; the freedom from self-blame and parental overprotection; the children's enjoyment of each other's company and lessened sibling rivalry; the enjoyment of music, games, and sports; the freedom from being word bound; and the physical style of learning.

I have also indicated the basic weaknesses of the disadvantaged which the school must try to overcome: Lack of school know-how, anti-intellectualism, and limited experience with formal language. Others should be noted: Poor auditory attention, poor time perspective, lack of test-taking skills, and limited reading ability. The school must recognize these deficiencies and work to combat them. They are by no means irreversible, but even more important, because neglected, the positive elements in their culture and style should become the guidelines for new school programs and new educational techniques.

There are a number of reasons why it is important for schools to emphasize the positive:

It will encourage the school to develop new approaches and techniques appropriate for the cognitive style of the deprived.

It will enable children of low-income families to be educated without middle-class values being imposed on them.

It will stimulate teachers to aim high, to expect more and work for more from the children. It will operate against patronization and condescension, and against the inflexibility in the double-track system which prevents the deprived from ever arriving on the main track.

It will curb the school's tendency to overemphasize vocational, nonacademic education for children from low-income families.

It will challenge teachers who realize that they need not aim simply at bringing these children up to grade level but can develop new kinds of creativity.

It will make the school more democratic because different cultures and styles, existing side by side, will interact.

It will enable the teacher to see that both techniques such as role playing and audio-visual aids are useful in eliciting the special cognitive style and creative potential of deprived children.

It will lead to appreciation of slowness, one-track learning, and physical learning as sources of potential strength that require fostering. It will challenge the teacher to take special training in how to respond to these styles, how to listen carefully to one-track persons, and how to reward the slow learner.

READING UNREADINESS IN THE UNDERPRIVILEGED[5]

Huh? . . . unh-hunh . . . nuttin . . . naw . . . wuh? . . . 'cuz . . . unh-unh . . . sho!

Is this a readiness-for-reading vocabulary? Definitely not! Yet, unfortunately, these "words," with variations for emphasis and inflection—plus a few other one-word sentences and a generous sprinkling of vulgarities—comprise the speaking vocabularies of many culturally disadvantaged first graders. These and other strange noises that take the place of standard American English reflect the impoverished language background of these children.

Although listening, speaking, reading, and writing skills are only a part of the needs characteristic of language-handicapped children, they are a vital part. Without mastering communication skills, culturally disadvantaged youngsters can never unlock the doors that lead to useful, productive citizenship; they can never become first-class citizens.

The above is not to say that culturally disadvantaged children cannot communicate with each other. Some of them have developed "scat" language [using nonsense syllables in singing or talking] to a rather high level of fluency. Nonetheless, this scat talk does not belong to the worlds of books or of business— worlds which are foreign to these children. Thus, teachers need to approach English language instruction for these children as if they were teaching a foreign language.

[5] From article by Warren G. Cutts, specialist for reading, Office of Education, United States Department of Health, Education and Welfare. *NEA Journal.* 52:23-4. Ap. '63. Reprinted by permission.

The foreign language approach might be coupled with one used successfully by some teachers. They have used the analogy of work clothes, play clothes, and Sunday clothes to convey the concept to the pupils of a different language for a different purpose. Different occasions call for different modes of dress, they explain, and the same thing is true of language.

As inconceivable as it seems, some teachers expect mastery of reading and writing skills by children who reveal gross deficiencies in listening and speaking.

Obviously, children who lack readiness for reading in terms of their oral language development and background of experience must have a prolonged readiness program either in school or before they enter school. Six-year-olds who cannot talk coherently can scarcely be expected to begin reading as soon as they enter school.

Children whose language is limited to grunts and crudities need extensive experiences before they are ready for any formalized reading instruction.

If these children are to master the basic language skills of listening and speaking, they must have a wider range of experiences—both real and vicarious—than their more fortunate counterparts.

Such experiences should include listening to stories told or read by the teacher; taking field trips to parks, farms, zoos, airports, fire stations, and other points of interest; using and listening to tape recorders; hearing records; and seeing movies and filmstrips. In all these activities, the main objective is to provide pupils with opportunities for language experience. They must, therefore, have plenty of time to react to and talk about the things they have seen and heard.

Teacher attitude is extremely important in helping disadvantaged children. The teacher needs to realize that vocabulary and language concepts develop slowly. He must learn to accept each child as he is and to respect him as an individual. He must take nothing for granted and carefully check all his assumptions concerning the child and the child's experiences.

For example, the teacher should not assume that children are familiar with points of interest in their own cities or, indeed, within their immediate neighborhoods. Many culturally deprived children have extremely limited horizons; many have never traveled more than two blocks from home before entering school.

That children learn largely from imitation suggests another important consideration for the schools: Culturally disadvantaged children cannot be kept out of the educational mainstream without perpetuating the inadequacies that set them apart in the first place. Although culturally disadvantaged children generally cannot progress as rapidly as other children, they must have an opportunity to associate with them. (For the sake of over-all progress, however, probably no more than four or five disadvantaged children should be assigned to any one classroom.)

Whatever the school's approach, something must be done to overcome the handicaps resulting from cultural deprivation, particularly as it affects readiness for reading instruction. Otherwise, American teachers and administrators must be prepared to answer for the failure of an ever-increasing number of children to master the necessary skills of communication.

If the schools are to help the culturally deprived, I believe that a radical departure from typical educational procedures and instructional techniques is needed. One such innovation might be to reach down into the preschool years to provide these children with some of the experiences which other children typically have had before coming to school.

Such experiences might be arranged through special nursery schools and day camps. Adaptations might be made, for example, from the All Day Neighborhood Schools program of New York City.

Day camps and nursery schools can also provide an opportunity for teachers and others to work cooperatively with parents. This is important, for if parents are not brought into the program and shown how they can supplement the school's work, teachers and parents of culturally disadvantaged children may foster concepts that are diametrically opposed to one another.

Of course, all of this would call for a larger staff and for a greater expenditure of money than at present.

More and more educators are recognizing the importance of working with culturally disadvantaged children during the early formative years. School systems such as those of Dearborn, Michigan, and Quincy, Illinois, are now shifting emphasis from the junior high and high school to kindergarten and first grade. This shift is long overdue and should be extended downward until it reaches into the preschool years.

Culturally disadvantaged children must be helped to accept themselves and to realize, at the same time, that different kinds of language are appropriate as situations vary. They must come to understand that without better language mastery they cannot hope to bridge the gap which lies between themselves and profitable occupations—between second-class and first-class citizenship.

Culturally disadvantaged children have much to contribute to society. Many of them are talented in music, in art, in athletics, and in other fields, but few of them have had the opportunity to reveal these talents. Most of them must depend primarily upon the school as the socializing force that can help them to find their places as contributing American citizens.

School and preschool enrichment programs may never be able to compensate fully for deficiencies in the experience and training provided by the home. Nevertheless, such programs can go a long way toward overcoming the handicap of a poor start, and without such enrichment, culturally disadvantaged children are certain to show irreparable gaps in their learning and to fall hopelessly behind the rest of society.

THE PASS-ALONG [6]

The scene was a symptom. In front of a grade school last year in a great midwestern city, parents walked in a curious picket line. They carried placards declaring: "Teach our kids to read!"—teach them before you pass them along.

[6] From "The 'Pass-Along': A Sign of Danger," by Francis Keppel, United States Commissioner of Education and former dean of the Harvard Graduate School of Education. New York *Times.* p 73. Ja. 16, '64. © 1964 by The New York Times Company. Reprinted by permission.

Here, in one city, was an attack against a practice of discarding standards, of passing children along from grade to grade whether or not they are qualified. What triggered the picket line was a guarded record sheet of reading achievements that had somehow reached the parents of an eighth-grade class. It showed that out of the entire graduating class, more than half the children were rated from fifth-grade down to second-grade level; that 80 per cent had failed to reach standards of eighth-grade reading. And yet all these children were quietly passed along.

The school where this took place was in the heart of the great city, and the children were Negroes. But the line that set them apart was not color alone. Elsewhere in the city are white children who are no less lacking in basic academic skills, who are similarly passed along. Elsewhere across the country are other cities, other schools like this.

Dangerous Flaw

The "pass along" school brings to focus a little-acknowledged but dangerous flaw in American education. In such schools we are failing to meet the challenge of young Americans who, on one hand, are difficult to teach and, on the other, are most in need of educational opportunity.

These are the youngsters of poverty, of the compacted slum areas of our cities, who are living apart from, and outside of, the most prosperous period of American life. At a time when education and skills are indispensable to economic and social achievement, they become high school dropouts because they find neither success nor stimulus in our elementary and secondary schools. Moreover, while their numbers are large and increasing, our efforts to improve their lot remain largely ineffective.

One reason for our failure to come to grips with the "pass along" generation is our habit of applying vague and general labels to these children. We call them "culturally disadvantaged" and "deprived," "socially underprivileged" and "handicapped."

A second reason for our neglect of the substandard schools is our failure to develop and use meaningful comparative criteria of achievement. We need to measure the achievement of our schools on a broad basis, from city to city and state to state. . . .

There is no need for these children to remain uneducated. But if we mean to succeed, we must begin to employ our knowledge through concerted funds and purpose.

Clearly, this effort will call for a new degree of candor on the part of the nation's school systems. Today there are few cities where the facts have been made available. And without facts, there is little prospect of finding solutions.

One city, however, has recently and commendably removed the cloak of silence from this area of acute need. The New York City Board of Education has boldly opened the records of achievement in central Harlem schools to public scrutiny. Among those who have examined the record is a study group called Harlem Youth Opportunities Unlimited. The results of its study . . . reveal a picture of intolerable educational neglect that can be duplicated in most of our largest cities.

Harlem Findings

Consider, for example, these findings in the elementary and junior high schools of central Harlem:

In the third grade, central Harlem pupils are fully one year behind the achievement levels of other New York City pupils. By the sixth grade they have fallen nearly two years behind; by the eighth grade they are about two and one half years behind.

About three fourths of the pupils in the central Harlem junior high schools are performing below grade level in both reading comprehension and word knowledge. In no junior high school here is the proportion of underachievers less than 70 per cent— and in some schools it is more than 80 per cent.

The pattern of test and IQ scores shows that education in central Harlem is marked by massive educational deterioration. The longer pupils are in school, the greater is the proportion who fall to meet established and comparative norms of academic competence. By the eighth grade, the gross damage has been done and acceptable grade levels thereafter are never attained.

Teachers Needed

From its extensive study of test results, the Harlem organization adds fresh coals to the fire over substandard schools.

The Harlem youth study, however, places far less stress on the economic and social environment of the child and far more on the educational environment he finds in the school itself. In central Harlem, the study observes, school teachers are the least experienced of any in the New York public school system. And they are particularly inexperienced in coping with the particular problems of the disadvantaged. . . .

This argument is now receiving increasing support in many quarters—that the education of slum children today confronts the nation with a clear and present emergency; that the challenge, now unmet by the cities and states, calls for specific Federal action.

John Kenneth Galbraith, Harvard professor, former Ambassador to India and author of *The Affluent Society* has called for "an attack on poverty by what I would judge to be the most effective single step that could be taken."

Professor Galbraith provocatively suggested that an emergency education program be undertaken in 1964:

Why don't we select . . . the hundred lowest income counties (or in the case of urban slums more limited areas of equal population) and designate them as special educational districts. They would then be equipped . . . with a truly excellent and comprehensive school plant, including both primary and secondary schools. . . .

Then, in the manner of the Peace Corps, but with ample pay, an elite body of young teachers would be assembled . . . tough and well-trained enough to take on the worst slums, proud to go to Harlan County or to Harlem. In the year following, we would proceed to the next most abysmal areas. . . .

Professor Galbraith's solution, one among many possibilities, may sound extreme. But it may well take measures as bold as these to clear the atmosphere of delay and excuses—and to get on with the major business of raising the level of education in our neglected city slums.

Unless we do, the problem will surely get worse.

If we fail to act—to live up to our ideals of universal education and equal opportunity—today's growing emergency will become an explosive social problem endangering our society for generations to come.

IV. LITERACY CAMPAIGN FOR THE UNITED STATES

EDITOR'S INTRODUCTION

The current national concern over poverty in the United States has heightened awareness of the plight of our under-educated citizens. As the preceding two sections of this book have pointed out, there are tens of millions of Americans whose lack of adequate education and literacy abilities puts them at a grave competitive disadvantage in our economy. There are more millions now in the schools ready to join this disadvantaged group. This section deals with some of the steps now being taken to combat undereducation in adults and to counteract the handicaps encountered by underprivileged young people.

The first article reviews the development of literacy campaigns in this country, noting that the United States Army, in World War II, was the first government agency to attempt large-scale anti-illiteracy programs. The article also comments on the relative dearth of school courses geared to train adult Americans today in basic literacy skills.

This is not to say that nothing is being done at the national and local levels. As Roy Minnis, of the United States Office of Education points out, the Federal Government has designed many different programs to fight poverty and undereducation. Of particular importance is the Manpower Development and Training Act, which offers additional schooling to youths who cannot benefit from occupational training because of their inadequate education.

Educating those who have already left the schools is only one part of the problem facing the nation in the drive against illiteracy. Another aspect is helping the millions of children who come from culturally deprived backgrounds and who stand a good chance of forming the undereducated of tomorrow—unless they are aided. Dr. Frank Riessman reviews some of the practices that have been developed in school systems to meet the special needs of this underprivileged group. The next articles speak of various kinds of school programs which have been designed to overcome the handicap of cultural deprivation. These programs range from preschool plans for slum children to a Higher Horizons program which attempts to kindle intellectual interests among older school children.

Not all of these programs can be expected to work out perfectly. There are numerous instances of failure. But there are also heartening numbers of successes. It is a beginning.

ELIMINATING UNDEREDUCATION [1]

Despite devotion to the democratic ideal of a literate population—the principle on which development of the public school system was based—little was done to eradicate pockets of adult illiteracy until recent years. A national conference on the illiteracy problem, called in 1924 by the General Federation of Women's Clubs, the American Legion, the National Education Association, and the United States Bureau of Education, produced little concrete action.

Two New Deal agencies—the Civilian Conservation Corps and the Works Progress Administration—provided a limited amount of literacy instruction to young adults during the 1930's. But national concern over illiteracy was not really stirred until World War II, when its bearing on national manpower needs became apparent. [As the authors of *The Uneducated* noted in 1953] "It was the large-scale screening of the younger male population consequent to the passage of the Selective Service Act of 1940 that turned a local and isolated fact into a national problem." The United States Army became the first government agency to undertake a major anti-illiteracy program.

[1] From "Illiteracy in the United States," by Helen B. Shaffer, staff writer, Editorial Research Reports. *Editorial Research Reports.* 1, no 17:339-42. My. 1, '63. Reprinted by permission.

Army Classes for Illiterates in World War II

The Army for a time accepted draftees of limited educational attainment so long as they could understand "simple orders given in the English language." Difficulty in training poorly educated recruits, however, led to a tightening of standards in May 1941; only those who possessed "the capacity of reading and writing the English language as commonly prescribed for the fourth grade" would be taken in. Growth of the demand for military manpower after Pearl Harbor then forced liberalization of the rule; each induction station was authorized to accept illiterates up to 10 per cent (later 5 per cent) of its daily quota. In June 1943 the literacy standard was virtually abandoned. All registrants who had not completed high school were examined, and illiterates who proved capable of serving after special training were inducted.

Special training units for illiterates and for those unable to speak or understand English had been set up as early as 1941. Such units were "handicapped by the lack of central direction, by the paucity of competent civilian instructors, and by the heterogeneity of the trainees." After the policy change of June 1943, the Army developed an efficient graded school system for illiterates, staffed by a large number of qualified civilian instructors. The goal of the special training units was to bring recruits up to at least fourth-grade levels of reading and number work so that they could "comprehend bulletins, written orders and directives and basic Army publications, . . . understand their pay accounts and laundry bills, conduct their business in the PX . . . [and] understand in a general way why it was necessary for this country to fight a war against Germany, Japan and Italy." The course ran for 120 days, but many of the pupils were graduated after a much shorter time; few had to stay in class more than 90 days. In all 255,000 soldiers—85 per cent of those enrolled—were graduated from special training units. . . .

Dearth of School Courses for Illiterate Adults

No civilian program of the magnitude of the Army effort in World War II has been undertaken. The country's public school systems have not found it possible to take on the task of educating illiterate adults on a large scale. . . . [A 1958-1959 survey revealed that] virtually all the literacy courses [offered by public school systems] were in cities with populations of more than 25,000; literacy instruction in rural areas where there were large numbers of illiterate adults was practically nonexistent.

Certain obstacles stand in the way of improving literacy skills of adults in civilian life which the wartime Army did not have to face. A primary problem has been to motivate those in greatest need of literacy education to take the courses available. Some illiterates are so involved in the multiple problems associated with their condition in life that they will not voluntarily enroll in literacy courses. Many illiterate adults are embarrassed by the thought of going back to school; others have taken pains to try to hide their deficiency from associates and are ashamed to be exposed.

According to former United States Commissioner of Education McMurrin, many efforts to educate illiterate adults have failed because materials and methods for teaching children were used. Effective teaching of adults was said to require special types of materials rather than the standard readers of primary grades. McMurrin testified last year that there were few teachers who "understand adult interests and needs and who can approach adults with an adult psychology." One of the purposes of the adult basic education provisions of the omnibus education bill now pending in Congress is to enable universities and other institutions of higher learning to develop specialized courses of training for teachers of adult basic education and for supervisors of those teachers.

McMurrin told the House subcommittee that only nineteen states had one or more professional staff members concerned with the entire spectrum of adult education, and that New York was the only state which had a professional staff member devoting full time to adult programs in literacy and other elementary subjects. "Any adequate program to reduce adult illiteracy," he said, "must include support for an administrative and supervisory organization at state and local levels having the authority and the resources to plan and conduct classes specifically in basic educational skills."

Important strides in adult literacy education are nevertheless being made. A notable boost came with a policy decision . . . [in 1963] to permit instruction in the three R's where needed in programs set up under the Manpower Development and Training Act of 1962. That law made no explicit provisions for courses in reading, writing and arithmetic. But experience showed that many in need of job retraining were unable to pass aptitude tests for lack of elementary skills. A pilot project to demonstrate the effectiveness of basic education as a part of the manpower retraining program was established . . . [in March 1963] in the District of Columbia, where a majority of the area's 12,500 unemployed are functionally illiterate. . . .

Television is playing an increasingly important role in anti-illiteracy campaigns. Memphis pioneered a half dozen years ago in putting on a televised program, widely supported by community organizations, which was adapted from techniques used by the missionary-educator Frank C. Laubach in various parts of the world. The course, known as Streamlined English, makes use of an audio-visual approach, superimposing letters and syllables on associated pictures; the Laubach method is the one used in the Washington, D.C., manpower retraining course.

FEDERAL AID FOR THE ILLITERATE [2]

Illiterates are an invisible group. They are defeated and hopeless. They recognize that they are different from other Americans. Many are continually hungry. They do not know the ordinary community services of police, fire, electricity, automatic heat,

[2] From address by Roy B. Minnis, specialist, adult education, Office of Education, United States Department of Health, Education and Welfare, delivered in New York City, April 8, 1964, at a conference on functional illiterates sponsored by the American Book Publishers Council and the American Textbook Publishers Institute. Text from *Wilson Library Bulletin*. 38:844-51+. Je. '64. Reprinted by permission.

health, and sanitation, all of which the rest of us take for granted as a right of an affluent society. They tend to be antischool, antiofficial, anticommunity, antiwork. They often resist personal involvement, religion, and feel totally pessimistic about their future place in society. Yet even with this negative set of attitudes they need not continue to be permanently ignorant or uneducated. Their own adult experiences can provide a base on which their training can be built. The research work carried on in Chicago for the training of illiterates and the experience of creative projects such as one recently completed in Norfolk, Virginia, just to mention two examples, indicate that the case is not hopeless nor are the solutions of educational problems unattainable. For the future of this country each undereducated adult must be identified, be placed in an environment where he can enjoy successful learning experiences, be educated with basic skills and be trained occupationally to take a place as a productive member of society.

The public education agency must take the lead, and engage in a partnership with other community agencies. Their common goal is to educate those who now play so little a part in the American system. The need for partnerships at all levels, state, Federal, interagency, and so on, will underlie all the remarks I will make in this paper. My purpose is to describe the various Federal programs which have or will have impact on the problem of poverty and undereducation. First we will look at the acts, the laws which have already been passed:

Manpower Development and Training Act

The MDTA was amended during the last few days of 1962. It is an active *partnership* between the Department of Labor and the Department of Health, Education and Welfare. Undoubtedly the greatest contribution at the national, state and local levels has been the communication, the discussion of issues, the establishment of a working relationship between the employment service and the school establishment. The amendments to the Act provide for two attacks on undereducation. First, it provides for "further schooling" for unemployed youth, seventeen through twenty-one, who are unsuitable for occupational training because of inadequate education and, second, basic education for adults without the educational skills to profit from occupational training. The length of training is not limited, but the allowance, payments to the trainee during the course of study, can be authorized for a period not exceeding seventy-two weeks. The maximum weekly allowance for the youth is $20 and for the adults $10 more than that authorized for unemployment compensation. During the first two fiscal years of this Act the total cost is borne out of appropriations by the Congress of the United States. The MDTA projects are developed locally or, in a few instances, at the state level.

Plans have been made to train fifty thousand undereducated persons the first year. After the first of July we expect that a sizable proportion of the young men referred to the "Youth Programs" will come from the ranks of undereducated youth rejected by the Selective Service.

Publishers, teachers, and librarians should be aware that the selection and purchase of the instructional and supplementary reading materials to be used for projects under the Act are handled by the project initiator, local or state educational agency.

Curriculum guides are now being developed in the Adult Education Branch of the Office of Education with the help of six consultants. The development of this curriculum material for MDTA projects under the auspices of the Office of Education is an indication of one type of *partnership* among the Federal, state and local educational establishments.

Community Work and Training Program

The Community Work and Training Program comprises amendments to the Social Security Act and is administered in the Welfare Administration of the Department of Health, Education and Welfare. Here welfare and the educational personnel within a single department engage in another type of cooperation. The intent of the amendments is the provision of basic education and occupational training for certain persons on welfare. Welfare payments are continued to enable these people to achieve enough education to qualify for employment and thus be eliminated from the welfare rolls.

The program can best be described by reviewing the experience in one state, Illinois. During the closing days of the 1963 legislative session the Illinois State Legislature passed an act authorizing a cooperative agreement between the State Department of Public Assistance and the State Department of Public Instruction to identify educable welfare recipients and refer them to their local school systems for basic adult education and/or occupational training. The amount of $4 million was appropriated for a two-year period. The State Department of Public Instruction began work immediately with the schools to develop adult education programs at an elementary level. The complete instructional cost is borne by the appropriation and the local school district is reimbursed for the costs as expended. Three out of every four dollars appropriated are derived from the Community Work and Training monies administered by the Welfare Administration of HEW. The magnitude of the program can be demonstrated by noting that between six and seven thousand persons are now enrolled in basic adult education programs in Chicago.

It should be pointed out again that the purchasers of instructional and supplementary materials are the local educational agencies with the advice of the state director of adult education. Many other states, notably California and New York, are about to embark on similar programs, and a number of demonstration projects are already being conducted in other states.

Vocational Education Act of 1963

The administration of the Vocational Education Act of 1963 is an example of a *partnership* among vocational educators at the Federal, state and local levels. To carry out the program effectively further cooperation must be realized between those engaged in vocational education and general education. As Commissioner

Keppel has recently stated, vocational and general education are no longer separate programs, but have become part and parcel of a total educational experience. He further stressed the essential need for both types of personnel to work together on the same educational team.

Among several other objectives, the Vocational Education Act of 1963 will provide programs at high school level to bring about a decrease in the dropout rate. These programs will meet the needs of the unemployed high school dropout, the high school graduate needing additional occupational training to become employed, and the adult who can become upgraded by learning new job skills. The Act covers programs of counseling and guidance for those who need such services, and provides education for persons with academic, socioeconomic or other handicaps which need to be alleviated if the recipients are to benefit from occupational training. Funds are also provided for the building of special vocational school buildings or vocational departments in established public institutions.

The purchasers of instructional and supplementary materials will be the local education system advised by state vocational supervisors or by the state vocational educational agency.

The Library Service Act of 1963

This Act extends library services beyond the residents of rural areas to those people living in urban areas. It also provides for the construction of library facilities and increases annual Federal authorization from $7.5 million to $25 million. The implementation of the Library Services Act implies the development of a *partnership* between the Library Services Branch of the Office of Education with the administrators of a state library agency and through them to regional and local libraries. The increase will augment the numbers of persons using public libraries and will facilitate the purchase of many more trade publications as well as instructional materials.

The purchasers of the books and materials will be the local libraries and, in some cases, regional and state libraries.

National Defense Education Act

Of particular interest is the amendment to Title VII of the NDEA which makes possible the funding of research and demonstration projects in educational media. This can lead to improvements in the publication of suitable materials. The contractees are educational institutions and nonprofit educational organizations. Both textbook and trade book publishers can work with such institutions and agencies on mutual problems.

Public Law 531

This Act permits the funding of basic research, demonstrations, developmental activities, and integrative reviews by state departments of education and colleges and universities. The Office of Education is encouraging the submission of proposals relating to the problems of the uneducated and undereducated. This is evidence of a *partnership* between state school systems and institutions of higher education with the Office of Education. Appropriate universities and/or state departments of education can again work with publishers in the development of major research and demonstration centers. Such centers would be concerned with the problems of developing both superior instructional materials for the undereducated and also a field testing service to provide a scientific evaluation of the uses to which the materials might be applied. Similarly, massive developmental programs must be instituted to assist in the preparation of easy and pertinent reading materials which can be processed and marketed by trade book publishers.

Area Redevelopment Act

Under this Act the Department of Commerce identified depressed areas where training programs up to sixteen weeks in length can be sponsored for adults. More important was the *partnership* developed under this Act at the national level between the Departments of Commerce, Labor, Agriculture, and HEW. The Act provided an excellent testing ground for ideas which were incorporated in the Manpower Development and Training Act and for concepts which are to be found in the Anti-Poverty Program. The purchasers of instructional materials are the local project administrators.

Listed below are the bills currently before Congress which will affect illiterates.

Adult Basic Education Act

This bill has been approved by the Education Subcommittee of the United States House of Representatives and the full Education and Labor Committee, and was forwarded during the first session of this Congress to the Rules Committee. The provisions of this bill are not restricted to certain categories of the undereducated. Instead the bill is designed to attack the problems in a frontal manner by working through state departments of education to local school systems. It would authorize in its present form $70 million and build a Federal-state-local school system *partnership*. The purchasers of the instructional and supplementary materials would be the local school systems.

Appalachia

This proposal spotlights the eight-state area along the Appalachian mountains, one of the most depressed areas of the nation. In meetings with a Federal task force team in each of the states, it became clear that the number one problem was the low-level or complete lack of education by a large majority of residents. The major issue was the development of human resources. This bill is designed to approach the problem through the development of an interstate structure which will cut across state lines, utilizing the resources of many Federal, state and local agencies. The major benefit, as I see it, is the *partnership* being developed among Federal, state, and local officials and among the Commerce, Labor, HEW, Agriculture, Interior Departments and the Home Housing and Finance Agency within the Federal structure. Purchasers of materials would be the local education agencies.

Antipoverty Program

The President's Antipoverty Program [enacted into law in August 1964] will establish an Office of Economic Opportunities reporting directly to the President. . . . The "job corps" title will provide both education and vocational training in residential centers. Also proposed is a work-training program for unemployed youth, both men and women.

The Urban and Rural Community Action proposal provides funds for a 90 per cent Federal level funding to develop a cooperative *partnership* arrangement among the various agencies concerned within each community.

The section on family unity through jobs provides $150 million a year for a program which appears to be very similar in concept to the community work and training program now financed by the Welfare Administration of HEW. It would provide work, training, and basic education.

BRIDGING THE CULTURE GAP [3]

It is natural enough for educators to stress the liabilities, the deficiencies, of the underprivileged. These are the things that the teacher is confronted with all the time. The deprived child clearly is not happy at school, does not read well, appears unmotivated, is antagonistic to the teacher, possesses no well-formulated career plans, has no quiet place to study. These are the things that are easiest to see because they are on the surface. To see his strengths, and positive struggles, requires a deeper, more penetrating look.

Many people see only the negative environmental conditions that surround the disadvantaged, and they believe that this *is* the culture. They feel that it is democratic and liberal to "accept" this culture (as just another way of life). But understanding of

[3] From *The Culturally Deprived Child,* by Dr. Frank Riessman, Department of Psychiatry, Albert Einstein College of Medicine. New York City, formerly consultant for Mobilization for Youth, an organization dedicated to helping the undereducated. Harper & Row. New York. '62. p 112-27. Copyright © 1962 by Frank Riessman. Reprinted with the permission of Harper & Row, Publishers, Incorporated.

this culture must include a genuine appreciation of the positives that have arisen out of the effort, however insufficient at times, to cope with the difficult environment.

This is different from the standard view, which, by accenting deprivation, emphasizes weakness. In fact, one of the great difficulties with formulations like "culturally deprived," "disadvantaged," "culturally handicapped," "impoverished," and the like, is that they connote inadequacy, rather than present a rounded picture of the culture which would have to include strengths as well as deficiencies. We feel that our view is not only a fuller, more accurate, portrayal, but that it also constrains against snobbery and patronization. Weakness seen in the context of strength has a different meaning. It is difficult to patronize someone of whose strengths you are well aware. To the extent that genuine cultural understanding takes place, there will be improvement in the problems of rapport in the classroom, the guidance office, and the Parent-Teacher Association.

If possible, teachers and psychologists should try to become interested in the nature and substance of the culture of disadvantaged groups and to find elements in it that they like, rather than endeavoring to understand it merely for practical purposes. . . .

Another Style of Thinking

Deprived children are capable of developing abstract, symbolic thinking. They appear to develop this type of thinking in a slower, more indirect fashion; that is, they require more examples before "seeing the point." There is no reason to assume that gifted children have to learn rapidly, although this is the implicit assumption in our culture today. Some individuals take a long time to learn a few basic concepts, but when they finally do so, they may utilize these ideas in a thoughtful, creative fashion. Much more attention needs to be given to the *slow-gifted child*. The underprivileged child has a cognitive style or way of learning that includes a number of features that have unique creative potential: his skill in nonverbal communication (he is not wordbound), his proclivity for persisting along one line (one-track creativity), his induction emphasis on many concrete examples, and his colorful free associative feeling for metaphor in language, perhaps best seen in his use of slang. These potentialities, indigenous to his cultural heritage, must be fully explored in any program concerned with developing talent among underprivileged groups.

The New Reader

The general estimate of reading inability among school children is 15 to 20 per cent, while among educationally deprived children the disability estimate is as high as 50 per cent. The significance of reading cannot be overestimated because all too often the deprived child remains retarded in all other subjects due to his inability to read. Junior high school teachers with whom we have spoken insist that they have to spend a large portion of the term teaching reading before they can start serious work on the subject matter of the course they are supposedly giving.

The development of reading ability is particularly important for the slow physical learner, for it is the key to overcoming his academic deficiencies and anti-intellectualism. Perhaps the most effective technique with deprived children is to "externalize" the reading. They have to read about things that they see, feel, and do.

Results of a three-year research program conducted at the University of Michigan indicate that three fourths of the first-grade children who "can't" learn to read may be helped by special attention and instruction. "In the average first-grade classroom of thirty pupils, there are eight 'can't' or children who do not make normal reading progress in the early grades. Six of the eight may be helped to overcome their problems," says Donald E. P. Smith, director of the University's Reading Clinic.

There is a great need for readers and materials more attuned to the experiences and problems of deprived groups. The textbooks now used in the school present predominantly middle-class illustrations, rarely concerning themselves with problems or heroes (e.g., Willy Mays) of the disadvantaged.

The problem goes deeper, however, than revising the readers for disadvantaged children. Leacock points out that what is needed is "a more reality-oriented program for all children." She states that:

A critical look at basic readers from the viewpoint of their discordance with "lower-class culture," reveals at a second look a discordance also with what is real experience for most middle-class children. One might ask how typical *are* Dick and Jane, or more important, how meaningful are they and their neat white house in the suburbs to children whose world includes all the blood and thunder, as well as the sophisticated reportage, of television. In what sense do Dick and Jane even reflect middle-class *ideal* patterns in the contemporary world? That such textbook characters help form ideal patterns in the early years is true, but does this not only create a problem for children, when the norms for behavior Dick and Jane express are so far removed from reality? One can even play with the idea of cultural deprivation for middle-class children, since home and school join in building a protective barrier between them and so much of the modern world; and one can wonder what the implications of this protection are for their mental health. Certainly such readers do not arouse interest in reading, which develops in spite of, not because of, their content.

It would be an exciting idea to have primers which deal more directly with people and events which arouse the emotions of sympathy, curiosity and wonder in children, texts which recognize whimsy as important in the building of values, which accept the adventurous hero as a valid character for children to respond to, which deal with the "child's world" as reaching from home and family to the moon. What contrast to the vapid amiability of Dick and Jane! And how important to have basic readers in which some children live in white houses in suburbs, but many more, equally important as human beings, live in tenements or apartments, or on farms, in the West, the North, the South, so that all children can read about all others, and, as Americans, get to know their world as it is. Nor, it should be added, is the same purpose served by a mechanical translation of Dicks and Janes to other places and periods in upper-grade readers. [Eleanor Leacock, comment in "Minority Group and Class Status as Related to Social and Personality Factors in Scholastic Achievement," by Martin Deutsch, Monograph No. 2, 1960. Published by the Society for Applied Anthropology, New York. p 31-2.]

A Specialized Teacher Education Program

Steps should be taken to reorganize teacher education in the colleges, where, by and large, it is predicated on middle-class norms. Courses currently given should be recast, and new courses about the teaching of the educationally deprived should be introduced. . . .

Future teachers have to understand that the problems encountered in teaching the underprivileged are not due simply to crowded classrooms or poor teachers. These factors play a role, but the important lesson the prospective teacher must assimilate is that teaching deprived children is a special problem requiring special knowledge. In many cases, teachers and administrators lack the basic theory for understanding the problems of the deprived.

There is a real need for a specialized teacher education program directed toward preparing teachers and administrators for working with underprivileged children. This program should be interdisciplinary, enabling education majors to integrate courses in many fields, such as applied anthropology, sociology, political science, economics, and psychology. Education training would thus be greatly broadened as well as intensified. The program should also be urban-centered, that is, concerned with problems of urban migration and redevelopment. It ought to include an intensive understanding of the nature of the city as viewed by the urban sociologist, the housing expert, the student of government the economist, and so on. The students might be required to select courses from a list such as the following: minority groups, delinquency and criminology, municipal government, social psychology, applied anthropology, urban sociology, Negro history, labor economics, labor history, and industrial psychology. If possible there should be paid internships for selected students who would work in underprivileged communities for one day each week with ministers, social workers, newspaper writers, and other leaders of the community. A special workshop, directed toward integrating the program and discussing the culture of the various minority groups in detail would be crucial for this type of project.

Knowledge and understanding of the deprived cannot come from courses and books alone, although we should not underestimate their value. *Experiences* can be particularly valuable, especially when they are carefully discussed and absorbed. Such experiences might include visiting PTA meetings, community centers, schools or classes where some of the problems have been dealt with successfully, fraternal groups and social clubs. Future teachers should have the opportunity of observing and talking with children from a deprived background who are now doing well in the school. (A special in-service program for school principals would be advisable because of the extremely important roles they play in establishing the atmosphere of the school and in teacher selection.) . . .

Teaching Machines and Programed Learning

There is a great need for increased utilization of teaching machines and programed, "automated" learning for deprived children, especially in the classes for "slow learners," and in the early stages of transition to the school. Teaching machines can also be used most effectively at the preschool level.

Special educational programing can be geared to the culture and thinking of the deprived child. Since the child can proceed at his own rate, there is less chance for the development of shame or anxiety on the part of the slow youngster. If a child moves from one school to another he takes his program with him. Moreover, teachers who have great difficulty adapting to the style of the underprivileged child can use the specially designed program as a base.

There are a number of other advantages for the deprived youngster: the "programing automates teaching by breaking information into small, sequential steps that can be exhibited one by one in a machine (or page by page in a book). The program writer is compelled to use the utmost logic and clarity." This step-by-step approach fits in very well with the inductive, careful style of the educationally deprived slow learner.

Questioning the student at each step, riveting his attention and rewarding him—immediately and continually with the satisfaction of being right, is again especially attuned for the unconfident learner who, in the early stages at least, needs "fast reinforcement."

The test-taking deficiencies of the underprivileged can also be overcome through the programing, as the test format is utilized without the disturbing competitive overtones of most school tests. The individual is striving for mastery of the program at his own pace; he is not competing directly against other children.

Lastly, the mechanical, gadgety, game-like character of automated learning is likely to have special appeal for the physically oriented, underprivileged youth.

A Peace Corps for the Deprived

Much fanfare is being given to the Peace Corps, in which young people serve as diplomatic representatives and technical aids in foreign lands. This is a splendid idea, but one which is not likely to favor the educationally deprived youngster. What the government can do for the deprived lies largely in the field of education, especially higher education. During World War II, the ASTP (Army Specialized Training Program) sent to college many underprivileged young men who would never otherwise have had this opportunity. This was a successful program, and with the current expansion of military functions there is no reason why it could not be resurrected. The army might also increase its vocational training program at the less advanced, noncollege level, as this is particularly attractive to disadvantaged youths who frequently enlist to learn a skill for which they could not afford to pay in civilian life. Few things are more effective in combating delinquency than job preparation and education with an eye to the future. The aimlessness which characterizes so many young people could, to some degree, be counteracted by a developed educational program. This, of course, need not take place in the military services alone. An expanded Government scholarship aid program for the needy would play a tremendous role also.

Research Agenda

The need for intensive research concerning the disadvantaged child is considerable. We need to know much more about the various dimensions of his mental style. We need better instruments to uncover his hidden intelligence. We need new and more appropriate personality tests to assess his character. . . .

There is a great need for centralization of research about the teaching of the deprived. On the simplest level, teachers with a demonstrated flair for successful instruction of deprived children should be observed and their practices analyzed. On a more ambitious level, experimentation in teaching practices should be set in motion.

NEW BOOKS FOR THE SLUM CHILD [4]

The lower-class, slum-dwelling child, "culturally disadvantaged" or "socially deprived," as he is currently called, has at least three particular reading problems that call for new kinds of books. First, it is shown, he cannot read well. Usually he falls steadily behind the expectancies for his school grade—norms, it must be said, that have been set for middle-class children. Second, he finds few of the books presently published in any way related to his day-by-day slum life. If he is a Negro or of Latin descent, which is more than likely, the books he sees seem even more remote, since they offer few, if any, dark-skinned heroes with whom he can identify. Third, if this child somehow has grasped the vision of life away from the blight of slum existence, he seldom finds among the books he can read a chart of directions for his anticipated upward social flight. So far the severe restrictions on his social mobility have produced in him a combination of chronic aggression and negativism, displaced hostility, repressed guilt and inferiority feelings, and irrational anxieties. The need for new and radically different books, to meet these three areas of need, is therefore critical.

[4] From article by Patrick J. Groff, associate professor of education, San Diego State College, California. *Wilson Library Bulletin.* 38:345-8. D. '63. Reprinted by permission.

The first kind of book—mature in interest level but very readable—has already appeared in increasing numbers of late. Such books usually have been innocuous enough in content to be inoffensive to racial segregationists both North and South; and, of course, they have been eagerly accepted by teachers of the many slum children who are retarded in reading. The need for these high-interest easy-reading books remains, as Dr. James Conant makes clear in *Slums and Suburbs*, but their value is limited. For while they are often adventuresome, suspenseful, or informative, their restricted content has little relation to the actual life and problems of the slum child.

The Invisible Man

The need for books to meet the second reading problem becomes apparent, therefore. The need can, perhaps, best be seen from a survey of the more widely used basal reading textbooks, such as the one on which Otto Klineberg reported in *Saturday Review* (February 16, 1963). Mr. Klineberg confirmed the opinions of many others that the life of the children portrayed in these readers is far removed from that of the slum child. The disadvantaged child has never experienced life in the new, clean, orderly, suburban homes of these readers, nor has he enjoyed their many pets and toys, numerous trips, and friendly, helpful relatives and neighbors. Here there is no observable poverty. Father has a well-paid, white-collar job, a dominant, respected role in the family. Everyone speaks standard English. No personal tragedy or conflict mars the serenity of this ideal setting. Above all, the scene is carefully laid in a segregated neighborhood of white people of North European origin, a neighborhood into which Negroes are obviously not allowed. Of course, this "nonexistence" of the black-skinned man perpetuates the myth of Negro invisibility, as Ralph Ellison has described it. The net effect of these books, as Klineberg sees it, is to strengthen the ethnocentric attitudes of the white child, while the dark-skinned slum child sees himself as an outsider, and an inferior. . . .

It is apparent, moreover, that if all racial barriers to social advancement were suddenly removed there would still be few jobs available to most parents of slum children because of their inadequate training. The new books should provide both motivation and practical advice by articulating school life and job preparation for the slum child. They can show him how to make a smooth transition from school to job, how to get into a labor union, how to be the first hired and the last fired (rather than the other way around, as now obtains). They can show the effects of being a burden on the community as opposed to the satisfactions of self-dependence. They should indicate concretely how command of language functions in job success and in social mobility.

The need for books that stress the development of good health practices, including dental health, also have a high priority. It has been shown, for example, that the slum child visits the dentist only one third as often as do other children. Books to help combat the high rate of illness and nutritional deficiency are imperative. New books that would give information to older slum children on sexual matters . . . are also urgently needed if the rate of venereal disease and illegitimacy among these children is to be reduced. . . .

Living in segregation necessarily saps the self-confidence of the slum child and stunts the development of feelings of mutual support with others. The new books, in general, should portray the practical consequences of segregation and discrimination—illustrate that they are economically unsound and wasteful of human resources, as well as immoral. Specifically, they can teach the depressed slum child how to establish his self-esteem, how to change his self-image, how to establish friendship patterns, how to accept, understand, and sympathize with others. They should teach him how to establish personal bonds with the school and his community. Characteristically, the slum child is limited to a very restricted participation in the community beyond his neighborhood. Vistas to a larger life can be expanded through books. How to be accepted by his teacher, why he is punished and praised, and how he can be creative and yet meet the external requirements of the school and society are questions the new books can answer.

Higher Horizons

Although the new books, to communicate to the slum child, must reach into his present existence, it is clear that they should stretch beyond it as well. The third group of needed books would help accelerate the mobility of the slum child toward the middle-class world as racial barriers break down. The struggle now carried on through Negro demonstrations across the nation seems to be aimed precisely at tearing down the barriers that have limited their realization of the American Dream—the attainment of full-fledged membership in the middle and higher social classes.

As Allison Davis says in *Psychology of the Child in the Middle Class,* almost all the things we cherish in American life are the achievements of the middle-class person: care of property, careful child rearing, sacrifice of immediate pleasure for future advantages, a long and trying period of formal education, the development of complex, salable skills, the drive to achieve ever-increasing importance in one's occupation, personal independence, liberty, power over future events, and the prestige and acceptance by others that grow out of this. These values, combined with the Judaeo-Christian ideals of humanity and charity, can allow for maximum economic and cultural opportunity for all, and thus make it possible for society to utilize fully the contribution each member can make.

PRESCHOOL PLAN FOR SLUMS TRIED [5]

Inoculating slum children against the deficiencies that often lead to disaster in school may prove more effective and less costly than treating the deficiencies at an advanced stage, many educators now are convinced.

[5] From article by Robert H. Terte, New York *Times* correspondent. New York *Times.* p 73. Ja. 16 '64. © 1964 by The New York Times Company. Reprinted by permission.

Since much of the damage is already done by the time the child reaches school age, the Ford Foundation is sponsoring a series of preschool projects in New York, New Haven, Baltimore, Boston and Oakland, California, and in Pennsylvania to find an effective preventive.

The primary aim is to develop programs that will systematically introduce children from economically, physically and culturally restricted environments to the kinds of experiences and the ways of thinking that will enable them to do well in school. . . .

Worsens with Time

Studies of the culturally deprived child have shown that the longer he stays in school, the further behind he gets. . . . This progressive retardation or cumulative deficit begins to appear at the third and fourth grade when the educational program shifts from emphasis on the tool skills of basic reading, writing and arithmetic to content areas, which build on concepts and language not specifically developed in the earlier grades.

The middle-class child makes the transition and continues to develop, but the child of the slums begins to stumble. . . .

Among the influences believed to affect the child's ability to learn in abstract situations are the quality and amount of speech between parent and child, the variety of experiences provided by trips and visits, the kind and quantity of books and toys available, the amount of reading to the child and similar experiences.

Parents a Factor

In addition to developing programs specifically for the children in the academic realm, the projects sponsored by the Ford Foundation seek to involve the parents to improve their influences on the educational development of their children. They are also seeking more effective relationships between health and service agencies and the schools to provide better assistance to children and parents in other areas—such as health and family ability—that influence the child's school performance.

Because special education is expensive compared with regular education, it is hoped to develop cost-sharing arrangements between the various agencies and different levels of government, from the local to the Federal. . . .

While remedial programs at higher levels will have to continue—including such efforts as Higher Horizons and projects to reclaim potential dropouts—"investments at earlier age levels begin to appear far more promising than at later ages" [a Ford Foundation associate observed].

Remedial work is costly not only in dollars but in the lost potential of students. And the chances of rapidly developing a large enough supply of expert teachers to meet the need for such programs are considered negligible. With these facts in mind the foundation is stressing the prevention of the development of learning deficiencies through its grants for the preschool programs.

The New York project, in its second year, is under the direction of Dr. Martin Deutsch, director of the Institute for Developmental Studies in the department of psychiatry of New York Medical College.

One hundred and sixty preschool and kindergarten children are taking part in the study in eight experimental schools in Harlem and on the Lower East Side. Because of lack of funds only about half of the group will continue in the project through the third grade.

Both the New York City Board of Education and the Department of Welfare are cooperating in the project. Dr. Deutsch hopes to develop a fairly detailed "therapeutic" curriculum with materials and techniques for overcoming specific weaknesses in various intellectual areas where problems are found.

The Baltimore public school system has agreed that in the second year of its preschool program next year it will lower the age for school enrollment of children who are considered culturally disadvantaged. This will in effect make the program part of the general educational services offered to them.

Funds have been provided within a larger project for the Oakland Board of Education to experiment with the assignment of language arts teachers to preschool day care centers. And in New Haven, funds have been made available to the Board of Education for the organization of voluntary preschool centers in slum areas.

The Pennsylvania program is under the state's Council on Human Services, which includes the Department of Public Instruction and the State Welfare and Health Departments. A full scale study has been inaugurated in one school district, with a revised curriculum for the primary grades to be developed and articulated with the preschool and kindergarten classes. The five years from preschool through third grade will be developed as a nongraded program.

Seven additional projects in Pennsylvania will provide summer programs for preschool children, with follow-up programs when they enter school, and various smaller-scale projects. In conjunction with each of the state's programs there will be special programs of teacher training and coordinated community services.

COOPERATIVE EFFORTS IN DEPRESSED NEIGHBORHOODS [6]

"Have you seen their apartment? No child can study under those conditions."

"She doesn't ever visit the school to find out how her children are doing."

"They don't come to PTA meetings, or take advantage of our adult education program."

Such observations are familiar to many classroom teachers and other school staff members. The subjects of these comments are the large and growing numbers of culturally deprived parents and other adults who live in the inner city of large metropolitan areas.

[6] From "Teachers and Parents Work Together in Depressed Neighborhoods," by Gene C. Fusco, specialist for school and community relations in the Office of Education, United States Department of Health, Education and Welfare. *Senior Scholastic.* 44:13T-14T. Ap. 24, '64. Reprinted by permission from *Scholastic Teacher*, © 1964 by Scholastic Magazines, Inc.

These groups are presenting educators with urgent and compelling challenges.

In middle-class communities, well-educated, economically secure parents seek out contacts with school personnel. They are active in parent-teacher groups, and generally reinforce the school's efforts.

In depressed neighborhoods, on the other hand, the educational backgrounds and experience of many parents preclude them from holding good jobs. They are highly transient, disoriented to urban living patterns, and preoccupied with bare economic survival. They live in deteriorating and overcrowded dwellings, in which home life is often noisy and disorganized.

These parents tend to be suspicious of, or shy with, school staff members. They are reluctant to visit the school. And they are not prone to intervene with school officials on behalf of their children. The inability of these parents to reinforce and support instructional programs and services offered by the school is a severe obstacle to their children's achievement of academic success.

Since the importance of the influence of the home upon motivational and cognitive development of children is generally accepted, this aspect of improving the educational opportunities of deprived children assumes monumental proportions. How can teachers and other staff members help deprived parents understand the nature of the demands the school places on their children? How can these parents, with the help of the school, participate meaningfully in advancing the education of their children?

Early Intervention

By the time a child from a marginal cultural environment enters school, his development has already reached a point where it is difficult to provide him with compensatory experiences. Both the child's desire and capacity to succeed in school may have already been impaired. Some schools are making attempts at early intervention in the life of the child: preschool classes for both children and parents, organized home visits by classroom teachers and other staff members prior to school entrance, and various types of parent education sessions are practices being tried.

Preschool observation classes in Baltimore are designed to help parents learn to guide the development of their children in such a way as to better prepare them for the schooling experience. Participating mothers bring their children, ages two through five, to the class and watch them participate in a variety of activities planned and supervised by professional nursery school teachers.

These parents are active observers. They record their observations of the children's activities and behavior on forms provided for that purpose. During the latter part of the 2½-hour weekly session, the parents meet with the nursery teacher, who points out the child development principles underlying the activities they have observed.

In some schools in Philadelphia, school-community coordinators (carefully selected lay persons with leadership qualities who are held in high regard by their neighbors) serve as liaison agents between school and home. These coordinators conduct regularly scheduled visits to the homes of parents of preschool children. If both parents are employed, they visit the home in the evening.

The coordinators suggest ways in which parents can help their children make the transition from home to school. Depending on the need, coordinators emphasize the value of subscribing to newspapers and magazines, of making trips to the center of the city, of taking advantage of selected radio and TV broadcasts. They may even show parents how to read nursery rhymes to their children or themselves teach the children simple songs.

Staff members of an elementary school in Chicago have developed a series of parent clinics. Meetings are held in an attractive room where refreshments are served and name tags provided. Every effort is made to maintain an informal and relaxed atmosphere. The school staff, including the principal, classroom teachers, and pupil personnel workers, participate in a discussion of ways in which parents can prepare their children for school.

Parents are encouraged, for example, to help their children learn numbers by counting knives, forks, and spoons at the dinner table. Parents are also urged to teach the children nursery rhymes and read them stories. Following the exchange among the panel members, parents move into small "buzz" groups to ask questions about their preschool children.

In-School Activities

Schools use a variety of methods for helping parents assume greater responsibility for the education of their children. In Detroit, a junior high school set up a four-week discussion group for parents to help them understand the school program and guide their children in planning for high school. Group meetings, one in the early afternoon and one in the evening, are held twice each week to accommodate parents.

In an elementary school district in St. Louis, evening meetings for parents are held in each school every semester to call attention to parent activities that can help children raise their level of motivation and academic achievement. The meetings culminate in a pledge of cooperation by the assembled parents. The parents' pledge includes a promise to ensure that their children will attend school every day on time, that they will provide their children with a dictionary and a quiet, well-lighted place to study at home; that they will give them suitable books frequently; and that they will visit the children's teacher at least once a semester.

In an elementary school in Baltimore, the school social worker identified a small number of parents with large families whose children had academic and behavior difficulties. Through intensive interviewing, she convinced the mothers in these families to commit themselves to attend a series of meetings twice each week at the school. Through the group meetings and individual conferences, the social worker, over a three-month period, attempted to influence those parent attitudes which she found to be hostile and suspicious toward school. She referred certain members of her group to appropriate community agencies which could provide specialized assistance.

Out-of-School Activities

The impoverished physical and social environment in the inner city offers a restricted range of experiences both to children and their parents. Families seldom leave the immediate neighborhoods to visit the downtown area. Some schools attempt to overcome such self-imposed restrictions by providing for both the parents and children organized excursions to places beyond the immediate neighborhood.

A Look Ahead

In Detroit, an elementary school staff makes contact with parents weeks in advance of bus trips scheduled for enrichment purposes. They help parents budget their money to save enough for the trip, and they prepare them for new experiences, such as eating in a restaurant or visiting a museum or zoo. Meetings held after the trip to determine parent responses to the experience aid school staff members in planning future trips.

In Philadelphia, a junior high school arranges Saturday parent-pupil bus programs. The trips are an outgrowth of activities in the classroom. Parents are invited to observe class sessions in which the trip activities are discussed.

In Chicago, an elementary school presents parents with a booklet entitled *Neighborhood Aids,* prepared by a committee of teachers. The booklet lists the names and addresses of health services, social service agencies, legal assistance agencies, nursery schools, counseling services, and recreational and cultural centers. Follow-up home visits by classroom teachers further guide parents in the use of the booklet.

Several developments, which may well become trends, are discernible. They include employing school-home coordinators, who attempt to interpret the school to the home and who inform teachers about home conditions influencing the child's school life; holding summer workshops for the school staff to sensitize them to, and inform them about, problems and opportunities in teaching in depressed neighborhoods; organizing intervisitation programs, which permit teachers to observe how other schools face problems similar to their own. Schools in depressed neighborhoods are also making greater use of pupil personnel workers, who must depend on teacher cooperation if they are to be effective.

Attitude Is Basic

Indeed, the *attitude* of the teacher toward low-income parents may well be basic to all other considerations for improving school-home relations. Alert teachers are aware that if they approach parents with low expectations of their ability and willingness to cooperate with the school, they will bring about a self-fulfilling prophecy. That is, parents will tend to conform to the behavior expected of them.

Experience shows that most parents are willing, even eager, to help their children succeed in school. Their motivation to perform this function is high; their knowledge and experience to carry it out are deficient. It is clearly up to school staff members to help such parents achieve a purpose they are only too eager to fulfill.

A SCHOOL FOR SLUM KIDS [7]

The fruits of a promising school-salvage experiment in the heart of Syracuse's Negro section will be shared with educators nationally wherever integration is a concern.

The Madison Area Project is a down-to-earth program designed specifically for culturally-deprived children who nonetheless may be "live wires." It is based on the principle that normal teaching methods and material are designed for middle-class children and must be changed for those from slum areas.

The curriculum and teaching procedures at Madison are modified to attract and hold the attention of underprivileged youth in an integrated but 90 per cent Negro institution of 2,600 pupils.

The hero of a favorite book among them is a Negro boy.

The experiment is being financed over a three-year period by $400,000 from the Ford Foundation, the city of Syracuse and the State Department of Education.

[7] From article by Otto Doelling, Associated Press correspondent. Text from *Long Island Press*. p 15. Ap. 25 '64. Reprinted by permission.

"Wings of the Future," says the sign on the drab, brick Madison Junior High School, center of the experiment. The slogan emphasizes the soaring aspirations of a school that two years ago stood on the threshold of becoming a blackboard jungle.

For a year and a half, the junior high school and two elementary schools that feed it have been the objects of a spirited task force of "change agents."

The task force includes specialists in teaching methods, psychology, social work, community relations and vocational guidance. They moved into the schools and tailored courses, methods and materials to the special needs.

Improvisation and personality groupings are main features. Teachers who once worked largely on their own now team to discuss how best to reach the pupils.

The program appears so successful that the schools will become training grounds next summer to groom teachers from throughout the nation for assignment in slum areas. Syracuse University is cooperating.

The Ford Foundation is providing $378,000 additional for the new teacher-training program. And the Madison Project, together with Syracuse University's Youth Development Center, has applied for a Federal grant of $415,000 for an experiment to determine through the project how racial integration in schools can best be achieved.

Dr. Mario D. Fantini, Madison Project director, hopes to demonstrate that his concepts can be applied effectively at schools in white neighborhoods that receive an influx of Negro pupils from a lower social strata.

"For true integration to take place," Fantini told a reporter, "we have to change the conditions within the school. Otherwise there will be desegregation but not integration."

"Integration doesn't happen automatically," he added. "You have to help it along."

The thirty-five-year-old native Philadelphian maintains that educational institutions lack the flexibility to change from within and that "change agents" must move into the school.

"Most teacher colleges train us to deal with middle-class children," said Kenneth Benjamin, an eighth-grade social studies teacher. "I never took a course on how to deal with deprived children. Why, it takes six weeks for a teacher coming into a school like this to become oriented."

In the past, teacher turnover at one point reached 80 per cent.

The teachers' lack of rapport with their pupils led to discipline problems and the rate of pupil dropouts was high, Fantini said.

Now the teaching staff has become stabilized and the dropout rate has declined drastically, he said.

SATURATION PLAN [8]

Dr. Calvin E. Gross, Superintendent of . . . [New York City] schools, is evolving plans for a "saturation program" to overcome educational deficiencies in areas of slums and racial imbalance.

The program has been the subject of a series of unpublicized high-level staff meetings since Dr. Gross's appointment to his post almost a year ago. It will incorporate the nation's most successful educational experiments, including the use of team-teaching, team mothers and small-group instruction.

Those who have been discussing the program are fully aware that it may be attacked by some civil rights groups as an attempt to create a northern version of the "separate but equal" doctrine.

Dr. Gross, however, insists that a saturation approach would offer superior schooling to children in the nonwhite slums and would be the only way toward real integration because it would raise the level of the slum areas and the potential of their residents. . . .

Operation in 1965

Dr. Gross believes that much of the financial support must come from outside sources such as foundations and possibly the Federal Government. Whatever funds may be offered by city and state, he is reported to believe, must be "new money" to assure that the project does not turn into just another reshuffling

[8] From "Schools Here Draft a 'Saturation' Plan for Negro Areas," by Fred M. Hechinger, education editor, New York *Times*. New York *Times*. p 1+. Ja. 5 '64. © 1964 by The New York Times Company. Reprinted by permission.

of existing forces and finances. He has told staff members that he wants "action to get the job done," not just more research projects.

The program is expected to be in operation in a substantial number of schools in the fall of 1965. No definite areas have been mapped out, since the extent of the program will depend on the funds available. But it is almost certain that sections of central Harlem and probably of the Bedford-Stuyvesant section of Brooklyn will be the first to be involved.

The key to the program is considered to be the plan to hand-pick the best teachers and to let them observe and study the best existing programs, experiments and university laboratory exploration. Then they are to be expected to take a leading hand in tailoring the education process to the specific needs of under-privileged children.

It is expected that selected groups of teachers will begin their training, observation and planning assignments next summer and during the 1964-65 school year. Some may be attached to other cities and suburban systems, while others may go to universities, settlement houses and other agencies.

Flexibility Is Key

While the key to the project is flexibility and the absence of any predetermined organizational pattern, it appears likely that the following devices may play an important part:

1. Team teaching, with teams consisting of expert teacher-leaders, student interns, specialists in reading, mathematics, art and other subjects.

2. Using team "mothers"—a category used successfully by Dr. Gross in Pittsburgh during his superintendency there. These "mothers" must live in the neighborhood of the school in which they join the teaching teams.

They are paid on an hourly basis, but become an integral part of both school and community life. Depending on their talents, they must be teachers' helpers or actually take part in simple instruction under the teachers' supervision.

Dr. Gross has talked also of using team "grandfathers" and "grandmothers" to build greater bonds between schools.

3. Instituting small-group instruction wherever it is necessary, not only as a remedial effort but also to prevent retardation before it sets in. Such instruction would be made possible, in part, by freeing some teachers through the use of television, teaching machines, recordings and other devices. The program also calls for the use of a larger number of expert teachers.

4. Permitting teachers in the early grades to free some children from all instruction other than reading for varying stretches of time, to assure competence in this basic skill and prevent frustration over inability to cope with the intellectual demands of school.

5. Working with parents and other adults, not only of school children, but also of preschool children. This may include the establishment of special kindergarten and nursery school facilities to give youngsters from deprived areas the conditioning for learning and understanding that children in more affluent homes are taught from infancy.

Dr. Gross's view that real integration will be obtained only by making the slum programs more attractive is supported by Dr. Kenneth B. Clark, psychologist at the City College of New York and director of the Northside Center for Child Development.

Key Figure in Court Fight

Dr. Clark is one of the original fighters for Negro rights in New York and was a key figure in the battle against the "separate but equal" doctrine that led to the Supreme Court decision of 1954.

Far from interfering with the aims of integration, he said such a saturation program would bring about real integration.

Dr. Gross has discussed the plan with top executives of a major foundation and has been given emphatic encouragement. He has also had unofficial talks about the project with Francis Keppel, United States Commissioner of Education.

While it is believed that initially no large-scale Federal support can be expected, a successfully initiated program would serve as a lever to persuade Congress that the urban slums need special education aid. This has been one of Mr. Keppel's persistent pleas.

HIGHER HORIZONS [9]

The greatest current effort to educate "culturally deprived" children is New York's "Higher Horizons" program, which started at Manhattanville Junior High School 43 in 1954, and has now been expanded to sixty-three elementary and junior high schools in the New York slums. Funds for the original program were given by the Committee on Integration, the College Entrance Examinations Board, the National Negro Scholarship Committee and the New York Board of Education, and the idea was to find college material now going to waste for lack of educational opportunity. "Only 4 per cent of the kids who went to . . . [Junior High School 43] ever went on to college," says Dan Schreiber, who was principal of the school when the program began. . . .

Nobody fudged on the choice of school—JHS 43 was about as bad as the city could offer. The measured IQ of the students averaged 82, a high proportion of the parents were on relief, virtually every child qualified for the free lunch program, and there was terrific turnover of both pupils and teachers. Truancy was high, and more than three fifths of JHS 43's graduates failed to graduate from high school. In 1953, when the groundwork for the project was laid, 105 graduates of JHS 43 were attempting the first-year academic program at George Washington High School, and 5 of them passed all their subjects, 2 with average grades of 80 or better. In 1960, 58 out of 101 JHS 43 graduates passed all their subjects on George Washington's academic program, and 28 had average grades of 80 or better. . . .

JHS 43 has produced some barely credible success stories. One boy with a measured IQ of 97 on entrance went off the top of the Pintner IQ scale at 139 before high school graduation, and won a

[9] From *The Schools*, by Martin Mayer, who visited some thousand classrooms in about 150 schools in preparation for this book. Harper & Row. New York. '61. p 124-8. Copyright © 1961 by Martin Prager Mayer. Reprinted with the permission of Harper & Row, Publishers, Incorporated.

scholarship worth $1,600, and a job worth $500, at Columbia University. Another, who started with an IQ of 74 (on the edge of retardation), four years behind in reading skills, was snatched from George Washington by New York University, with a $1,380 scholarship. . . .

Changes in the curriculum have been in the direction of greater emphasis on academic courses—about one half of the school now takes both algebra and a foreign language in ninth grade. There are also two "special" classes which complete the three years' work of junior high school in two. These classes, however, represent the pick of western Harlem and not just the talented kids from JHS 43's own neighborhood. . . .

Our first job with these kids [says Dan Schreiber] is the creation of a decent self-image. They are encouraged to think they can achieve, and they achieve. The opinion that a majority group holds of a minority group, in our experience, tends to make the minority group behave according to that opinion. So many kids are told, "You're a Negro—you can't move up." They come to believe it.

From the beginning, JHS 43's guidance program was unimaginably ambitious. The kids were taken on trips, first to the New York City colleges, engineering schools, pharmacy schools and hospitals, where they were shown all the facilities and—incidentally—saw Negroes and Puerto Ricans getting a higher education. They were introduced to the life of their city—taken to plays on and off Broadway (and received backstage, after performances, by Helen Hayes and John Gielgud, among others), taken to the Metropolitan Opera (where Nell Rankin received them backstage), sent regularly to concerts of the New York Philharmonic. At first they went to the Saturday morning children's concerts, but when Leonard Bernstein sold those out they shifted to the regular Friday afternoon series, to which the school bought sixty subscriptions. Schreiber was more than a little nervous about the shift—the Friday audience at the Philharmonic is New York's stuffiest, and these were, after all, slum kids; you couldn't be certain how they'd react. They leave school at lunchtime and go to the Automat near the Philharmonic to eat their sandwiches, and then they go to the regular concert. So far as Schreiber can find out, they love it.

Other trips took the kids to the Roosevelt home at Hyde Park, to Stratford, Connecticut, for the Shakespeare festival, to Washington Irving's Sleepy Hollow, to the rebuilt early American village at Smith's Cove. They came to know, for the first time, the city in which they lived—the commercial center and the financial market, the streets of good shops, the parks, the better residential areas. And they were told, over and over again, that nothing was beyond them.

The guidance staff was enlarged to a dozen people, and given a special room which was hung with college pennants and pictures of Negro and Puerto Rican professional men and women at work. Finally, the kids were taken on "dream college" trips to Yale and to Princeton. Schreiber called their employers (most of JHS 43's better kids have jobs on Saturdays), and asked for the day off; if the kids needed the money, he reached into a special fund at his disposal and paid them for the day. On Saturday morning these refugees from one of the nation's most blasted neighborhoods strolled the Gothic quadrangles of Yale and Princeton, saw how students lived, sat in on a class, visited laboratories, went to the local stationery stores and bought Yale and Princeton paper jackets to put around their own schoolbooks. In the afternoon, they went to the football game. "When they read the sports pages afterward," Schreiber says, "they always looked up what happened to *their* college. I don't know what books you read as a boy, but I read Frank Merriwell, Henry Barbour. I wanted these kids to have that sort of experience, too."

Reading was and is the most serious scholastic problem at JHS 43, and Schreiber tackled it directly. Every teacher was made responsible for reading in her classroom, and was told to devote at least ten minutes of every period to reading instruction. "Book Fairs" were held just before Christmas and Easter—featuring remainders, discount books and pocket books—to encourage the idea that books made good gifts. Merit badges were given to kids who read on their own—a "Reader" badge for six books, a

"Leader" badge for twelve. Oral reports were not required—each child could jot down something about his book on a three-by-five card, or draw a picture about it, if he wished. Teachers were told not to worry if a child cheated them once or twice: this was on the honor system. For most of the kids at JHS 43, it was the first time they had ever been trusted in anything connected with education; on the whole, they reacted well.

Not every child in the school was chosen for the Higher Horizons program. A battery of special tests was given—verbal and nonverbal IQ's, achievement tests in vocabulary and reading comprehension, mathematical computation and reasoning, information and understanding in various areas. Any child who scored average or above on six of ten criteria—one of which was grades and teacher recommendation—was accepted for the program. There were also a few others whose scores made an odd shape when plotted as profiles—children who were suspiciously better at paragraph comprehension than at vocabulary, at mathematical reasoning than computation—who were accepted by Higher Horizons at least until the reasons for the differences were established. One boy taken on that basis was the 74 IQ student who later won the scholarship to NYU: if the school had averaged out his "verbal" and "mathematical" score instead of examining the component scores, he would not have qualified. The essence of the plan was to give everybody a chance who might possibly succeed. About half the school got the chance, and about half of those took remarkably full advantage of their new opportunities. . . .

Higher Horizons costs an extra fifty dollars per child per year. "Twenty-five cents a day," says Dan Schreiber. "Three cents a class period."

FRONTAL ATTACK ON ILLITERACY [10]

For all his thirty-three years, Charlie had lived in a twilight world. Parts of his life were real enough—his mother, the num-

[10] From article by Jack T. Parker, assistant executive secretary of the National Association of Public School Adult Educators. In *Focus on Public School Adult Education;* third yearbook of the National Association of Public School Adult Educators. p 121-3. '63. The Association. 1201 16th St. Washington, D.C. 20036. Reprinted by permission.

berless jobs he'd had since he was nine, and now his wife and two youngsters. It was the gray parts he'd never been able to get used to. It was the "left out" feeling that bothered him. And it was a good many years before Charlie realized that he wasn't the only grown man who had never learned how to read and write.

One thing about it, though. Illiteracy had taught Charlie how to be a pretty good actor. He'd built up a bag of tricks that could fool most anyone into thinking he could read. When he first got married, he brought a paper home every night and sat leafing through it for close to an hour looking at the pictures or sometimes just staring at the biggest headlines and thinking. Forgetting his glasses was a pretty good excuse for getting out of reading things at work. And radio and television kept him up to date enough on the news to hold up his end of a conversation.

Of course, some people had to find out. When Charlie couldn't name any letters beyond the "E" on the optometrist's eye chart, the doctor found out. When he couldn't read the questions on a health insurance questionnaire, the plant personnel director found out. His wife confronted him with it when he couldn't fill out a credit application.

Charlie wanted to learn to read and write and maybe do a little figuring but he wasn't without pride. First of all he wasn't sure he could learn. Then, the thought of going into a school with a lot of strangers who would quickly see through his protective barrier was just too unnerving to consider very seriously.

So Charlie stayed in his twilight world and pretended some more.

There are millions of Charlies in the United States and only a relative handful are sufficiently motivated to break down their protective barriers.

But new hope for this problem is seen in *Operation Alphabet,* a TV literacy education series developed by the Philadelphia Public Schools' School Extension Division and sponsored nationally by NAPSAE [National Association of Public School Adult Educators]. Launched nation-wide in 1962, *Operation Alphabet* offers the illiterate the opportunity to learn basic reading and writing skills in the privacy of his own home and through the already familiar medium of television. As self-confidence builds, it is hoped that the barriers to formal education will crumble. There is evidence that this is happening.

In Philadelphia, enrollments in adult elementary education classes rose 25 per cent after the first showing of the series. In Cincinnati, enrollments rose 21 per cent.

That *Operation Alphabet* appeals to the nonreader is almost certain. Kansas City, Mo., a city that carefully followed NAPSAE's operational plan for OA, discovered that it was reaching 8,000 of its illiterates with the series. Kansas City has only 25,000 functional illiterates according to the 1960 Census. Thus *Operation Alphabet* reached nearly one third of its functionally illiterate population in a single, twenty-week operation.

Briefly, *Operation Alphabet* is a series of one hundred half-hour television programs on video tape. The tapes are offered to television stations without charge through a grant from the Annenberg School of Communications, University of Pennsylvania. NAPSAE publishes a *TV Home Study Book* which has one hundred printed lessons based on the televised lessons. The book reinforces and supplements what the learner sees and hears on his TV screen. The association also provides a packet of promotion materials designed to reach illiterates with information about the series.

The conscientious learner will reach or nearly reach a third-grade reading and writing level by the time he finishes the hundredth lesson. It is at this point that efforts should be made locally, via television and every other possible means, to get the learner enrolled in a formal education environment so that he can progress to the eighth grade and beyond.

About forty cities, including nearly all of the largest, have shown *Operation Alphabet* and some have scheduled a second showing. NAPSAE recommends at least two showings. Whether or not a third would prove valuable remains to be seen.

Meanwhile, Philadelphia is working on a second series to begin where the first ends and, hopefully, work up to the sixth-grade level. This series, too, would not be a substitute for formal instruction under the guidance of a trained teacher but, rather, a supplement and stimulant to it. . . .

Operation Alphabet is not a cure for the problem [of illiteracy]. Rather it is an approach to it and one of the best approaches at our disposal today. Philadelphia's adult education program, under the direction of Robert H. Coates, is a prime example of what a local community can do—through adult education—to attempt to solve a community problem. Its willingness to share its experience with the rest of the nation permitted NAPSAE to enter the picture as a stimulator, coordinator, and expediter.

Whether *Operation Alphabet* will significantly alter the illiteracy pattern in this country will not be known for many months, perhaps years. But the mere fact that NAPSAE is at the forefront of massive, frontal attack on the problem is encouraging. The fact that the association is *trying* new approaches to the problem is significant. And perhaps most important is the indication that fellow citizens of all the undereducated Charlies in this country are beginning to care—are beginning to show Charlie a way out of his twilight world.

RELATING REALITY TO EDUCATION [11]

One requirement for the continuation of our progress in education—in fact our progress as a nation—has become increasingly clear in recent years. We must find ways to break into the closed circle of failure and indifference to education which continues to afflict a substantial minority of our people. This we must do merely to have a *chance* to reclaim our disadvantaged and our

[11] From "Education: The Dawning of a Renaissance," address by Wayne O. Reed, deputy commissioner, Office of Education, United States Department of Health, Education and Welfare. The address was delivered January 14, 1964, at the Cherry Hill Conference, sponsored by the American Textbook Publishers Institute in cooperation with the Office of Education. Text from *A Conference on Developing Programs and Instructional Materials for Adult Basic Education and Job Skill Training.* The Institute. 432 Park Ave. South. New York, N.Y. 10016. '64. p 8-11. Reprinted by permission.

disaffected fellow citizens to economic competence and social identification. We know from experience that the circle is hard to break. Children of hopeless parents develop hopeless outlooks. Failure and apathy breed failure and apathy. But the circle can be broken and we know what it takes. It takes human concern, among other things, and it takes materials and methods that relate to the realities of people's lives, whether they be first graders or unemployed laborers. . . .

Literacy is something all of us take for granted—we achieved it so long ago in the dimly-remembered past. But literacy is the key to knowledge and thereby one possible avenue to social reclamation.

Literacy also can be the key to vocational training that will get a man or woman a job. We have seen recently in projects at Norfolk, New Haven, New York City, and many other places, that adults can learn auto mechanics, electronics, welding, drafting, masonry, carpentry, metal work, and other trades while greatly improving reading and writing skills. It is being demonstrated in more than twenty special projects that it is possible to recruit unskilled workers into training programs even when there are mouths to feed at home, and it is hard to take time out for training.

In the Norfolk project, for example, of the one hundred men who started the fifty-two-week program, ninety remained to receive their certificates. This represents a dropout rate of only 10 per cent compared to an average of 25 per cent to 40 per cent in other retraining programs. Findings indicated that the participants' achievement scores in reading and writing were pushed up two grade levels in six months. The Norfolk results demonstrated that incorporating the improvement of basic education skills as a means to learn vocational skills and thereby gain employment gives an adult the practical incentive to learn.

From recent experiences in experimental retraining programs —both for youth and adults—we know that lack of basic ability is not a principal cause in most of the cases of uneducated and unemployed persons. Circumstance—the lack or the denial of training and education—has placed the culturally deprived worker at a crippling disadvantage in our society.

This is a problem we can do something about, widespread though it may be. President Johnson has made it clear that education is a primary weapon in his declared war on poverty and despair. In an article in the . . . [January 1964] *NEA Journal*, the President emphasizes that "the quality and quantity of our education effort should be stepped up at all levels in an effort to help persons attain the background they need."

Evidence abounds on all sides that Americans are ready to launch sustained efforts to eliminate functional illiteracy as a cause of social isolation and economic incompetence. The job will not be easy. It will not be crowned with overwhelming initial success. In addition to a lot of money, it will require talented and understanding teachers, and an ample supply of well-designed instructional materials aimed at the needs of these particular students.

This is one of the important tests of our dawning renaissance in education. Will this renaissance continue to bloom with increasing energy and creativity, or am I too optimistic in reading the signs? Our destiny as a free people may well depend on fulfillment of this tentative promise for a new and pervasive commitment to education in American life. The commitment will be sustained and the renaissance advanced by the combined efforts of all segments of our society, and of our educational enterprise in particular.

We are on the threshold of new developments in the teaching-learning process that will increase rather than decrease the importance of teachers and of high quality instructional materials. Government can reflect the concern of the people and support more and better educational programs. The writers and publishers of educational materials are indispensable partners in sustaining the quality and timeliness of these programs.

BIBLIOGRAPHY

An asterisk (*) preceding a reference indicates that the article or a part of it has been reprinted in this book.

BOOKS, PAMPHLETS, AND DOCUMENTS

*American Textbook Publishers Institute. Conference on developing programs and instructional materials for adult basic education and job skill training; proceedings of a conference sponsored by the Institute in cooperation with the United States Office of Education at Cherry Hill, New Jersey, January 14-15, 1964. The Institute. 432 Park Ave. South. New York, N.Y. 10016. '64.
  Reprinted in this book: Education: the dawning of a renaissance. W. O. Reed. p 8-11.

Betts, E. A. Foundations of reading instruction. American Book Co. New York. 1950.

Brice, E. W. Education of the adult migrant. (Bulletin 1961, no 6) United States Department of Health, Education and Welfare. Office of Education. Washington, D.C. 20202. '61.

Conant, J. B. American high school today. McGraw-Hill. New York. '59.

Conant, J. B. Slums and suburbs; a commentary on schools in metropolitan areas. McGraw-Hill. New York. '61.

Council on World Tensions. Restless nations: a study of world tensions and development. Dodd, Mead. New York. '62.

Cutts, W. G. ed. Teaching young children to read. United States Department of Health, Education and Welfare. Office of Education. Washington, D.C. 20202. '64.

*Gardner, J. W. Excellence; can we be equal and excellent too? Harper. New York. '61.

Ginzberg, Eli and Bray, D. W. The uneducated. Columbia University Press. New York. '53.

Harrington, Michael. Other America; poverty in the United States. Macmillan. New York. '62.

Huntington Library. Mexico; the challenge of poverty and illiteracy. The Library. San Marino, Calif. '63.

Laubach, F. C. Thirty years with the silent billion: adventuring in literacy. Revell. Westwood, N.J. '60.

Laubach, F. C. and Laubach, R. S. Toward world literacy; the each one teach one way. Syracuse University Press. Syracuse, N.Y. '60.

Lewis, M. M. Importance of illiteracy. Harrap. London. '53.

May, Edgar. Wasted Americans; cost of our welfare dilemma. Harper. New York. '64.

*Mayer, Martin. The schools. Harper. New York. '61.

*National Association of Public School Adult Educators. Focus on public school adult education; third yearbook. The Association. 1201 16th St. N.W. Washington, D.C. 20036. '63.
    Reprinted in this book: Frontal attack on illiteracy. J. T. Parker. p 121-3.

Pan American Union. Inter-American seminar on literacy and adult education. The Union. Washington, D.C. 20006. '50.

*Passow, A. H. ed. Education in depressed areas. Teachers College, Columbia University. New York. '63.
    Reprinted in this book: The disadvantaged child and the learning process. M. P. Deutsch. p 163-75.

*Riessman, Frank. Culturally deprived child. Harper. New York. '62.

Robinson, F. P. Effective reading. Harper. New York. '62.

Smith, E. H. and Smith, M. P. Teaching reading to adults. National Association of Public School Adult Educators. 1201 16th St. N.W. Washington D.C. 20036. '62.

*UNESCO. World campaign for universal literacy. UNESCO. Paris. '63.

UNESCO. World illiteracy at mid-century: a statistical study. (Monographs on fundamental education—XI) UNESCO. Paris. '57.

UNICEF. Children of the developing countries. World Publishing Co. Cleveland. '63.

United States. Department of Health, Education and Welfare. Office of Education. Report of the task force on adult basic education; instructional materials and related media. The Department. Washington, D.C. 20202. Ja. '64.

*United States. Senate. Committee on Labor and Public Welfare. War on poverty; the economic opportunity act of 1964; a compilation of materials relevant to S. 2642; prepared for the select subcommittee on poverty of the Committee on Labor and Public Welfare. 88th Congress, 2d session. Supt. of Docs. Washington, D.C. 20402. '64.

Ward, B. A. Literacy and basic elementary education for adults; a selected annotated bibliography. (Bulletin 1961, no 19) United States Department of Health, Education and Welfare. Washington, D.C. 20202. '61.

PERIODICALS

ALA Bulletin. 57:1034-8. D. '63. Massive attack on illiteracy: Cook County experience; excerpts from address, July 13, 1963. R. M. Hilliard.

ALA Bulletin. 58:523-6. Je. '64. Broadening the experience of the culturally disadvantaged. Alexander Frazier.

Adult Leadership. 9:47-8. Je. '60. Illiteracy at the crossroads. P. C. Berg.

America. 97:342-3. Je. 22, '57. Educating for illiteracy? Sister Mary Denise.
    Reply: 97:413. Jl. 20, '57. M. C. Miller.

America. 97:663. S. 28, '57. Ignorance is no longer bliss; national commission for adult literacy. N. G. McCluskey.

America. 109:73-4+. Jl. 20, '63. Poverty U.S.A. B. L. Masse.

American Federationist. 69:23-4. Ap. '62. America's 8,000,000 illiterates.

*Américas. 10:6-10. N. '58. 10,000,000 U.S. illiterates. Eli Ginzberg.

Atlantic. 200:31-4. O. '57. Each one teach one; interview. F. C. Laubach.

Business Week. p 190+. Ap. 18, '64. Other side of affluence.

Christian Century. 80:901. Jl. 17, '63. Only $2 billion to end illiteracy.

Clearing House. 37:80-3. O. '62. Special language problems of the culturally deprived. W. G. Cutts.

Commonweal. 70:391-2. Jl. 31, '59. Disinherited. John Stanley.

*Commonweal. 71:175-7. N. 6, '59. Pool of ignorance. C. K. Yearley, Jr.

Coronet. 50:174-5+. S. '61. I was a high school drop-out! D. J. Giese.
    Same abridged: Reader's Digest. 79:203-7. D. '61.

*Editorial Research Reports. 1, no 17:327-44. My. 1, '63. Illiteracy in the United States. H. B. Shaffer.

Fortune. 69:118-19+. Mr. '64. Who are the American poor? E. K. Faltermayer.

Harper's Magazine. 222:46-52. Ap. '61. Good slum schools. Martin Mayer.
    Discussion: 222:8. Je. '61.

Higher Education. 18:7-10. S. '61. Education and national development. F. N. Hamblin.

*Illinois Education. 25:387-9. My. '63. Undereducation in our American society. E. W. Brice.

International Journal of Adult and Youth Education. 14, no 4:200-4. '62. Universal literacy in the development decade. Ella Griffin.

Library Journal. 89:1515. Ap. 1, '64. Cost of literacy. Eric Moon.

Life. 26:74+. Ap. 11, '49. One-man literacy crusade.

Life. 42:47. Ja. 28, '57. Big lift for illiterates; Memphis TV show.

*Long Island Press. p 15. Ap. 25, '64. School for slum kids. Otto Doelling.

*McCall's. 91:96-7+. F. '64. Illiteracy; the key to poverty! Bernard Asbell.

Minnesota Journal of Education. 42:9-10. D. '61. Education and social class. I. O. Miller.

*NEA Journal. 45:428-9. O. '56. Cost of adult under-education. R. A. Luke.

NEA Journal. 50:23-4. Ap. '61. Culturally deprived child in school. Morris Krugman.

NEA Journal. 50:29-30. My. '61. I could write only two words. P. T. Luebke.

NEA Journal. 52:17-20. Ap. '63. Great cities projects. Dorsey Baynham.

NEA Journal. 52:20-2. Ap. '63. Teaching the culturally deprived. Frank Riessman.

*NEA Journal. 52:23-4. Ap. '63. Reading unreadiness in the under-privileged. W. G. Cutts.

NEA Journal. 52:25-7. Ap. '63. Disadvantaged newcomers to the city. J. M. O'Hara.

National Parent-Teacher. 53:20-3. N. '58. Campaign against illiteracy. P. A. Witty.

New Republic. 149:7. O. 19, '63. Extreme situation; dropouts return to school. Paul Goodman.

New Republic. 150:5-6. Ja. 18, '64. Pilot lights; educating the under-privileged.
    Reply: 150:30. F. 22, '64.

New Statesman. 59:931. Je. 25, '60. Learning to read. M. E. Stewart.

New York Times. p 6. F. 16, '62. Education urged to aid unemployed.

New York Times. p 8. S. 22, '62. Study of relief cites illiteracy.

New York Times. p 5. F. 9, '63. Nigerian urges conscription to fight African illiteracy.

New York Times. p 30. My. 10, '63. Job-seekers told to get schooling.

*New York Times. p 18. Je. 2, '63. Brazil conducts a literacy drive. Juan de Onis.

New York Times. p 18. Je. 2, '63. U.N. seeks worldwide effort to teach 700 million illiterates. A. H. Lubasch.

New York Times. p 15. Je. 24, '63. Jobless taught skills and hope. J. D. Pomfret.

New York Times. p 49. S. 8, '63. Chicago project will aid youths. A. C. Wehrwein.

New York Times. p 19. D. 14, '63. Galbraith asks drive on poverty with top schools in poor areas.

New York Times. p 26. Ja. 3, '64. Dropout center opens in Harlem. Farnsworth Fowle.

*New York Times. p 1+. Ja. 5, '64. Schools here draft a saturation plan for Negro areas. F. M. Hechinger.

New York Times. p 46. Ja. 6, '64. Road to better slum schools.

New York Times. p 13. Ja. 13, '64. Volunteers sought for literacy drive.

*New York Times. p 73. Ja. 16, '64. The pass-along: a sign of danger. Francis Keppel.

*New York Times. p 73. Ja. 16, '64. Pre-school plan for slums tried. R. H. Terte.

New York Times. p E7. Ja. 19, '64. To help the poor. Marjorie Hunter.

New York Times Magazine. p 43+. Mr. 16, '58. Almost half the world's adults can't read. L. H. Evans.

*New York Times Magazine. p 13+. My. 24, '64. New lost generation: jobless youth. Michael Harrington.

Newsweek. 47:84. F. 6, '55. Sad state of literacy.

Newsweek. 50:76. Jl. 1, '57. Our backward adults.

Newsweek. 53:66+. Mr. 30, '59. Our illiterates.

Overseas. 2:6-9. Ap. '63. War against world illiteracy. R. W. Cortright.

*Overview. 3:33-5. O. '62. The illiterate American.
   Same condensed: Education Digest. 28:32-4. D. '62.

PTA Magazine. 56:17-8. D. '61. What's happening in education; what is the higher horizons program? W. D. Boutwell.

PTA Magazine. 57:11. O. '62. What's happening in education; culturally deprived children. W. D. Boutwell.

Publishers' Weekly. 185:38-50, 57. F. 17, '64. War on poverty; book publishing's role in adult education, job retraining; symposium; with editorial comment.

Publishers' Weekly. 185:32-43, 52. My. 4, '64. War on poverty: conference sponsored by American Book Publishers Council and the American Textbook Publishers Institute; with editorial comment.

Reader's Digest. 77:245-8+. O. '60. Higher horizons for our asphalt jungles. Lester Velie.

Reader's Digest. 81:99-102. N. '62. Who will weep with Willie McGee? Lester Velie.

Saturday Evening Post. 232:19+. N. 28, '59. World of the uneducated. H. G. Rickover.

Saturday Evening Post. 234:40-1+. F. 4, '61. Road out of the slums: Higher horizons project. C. T. Rowan.

Saturday Evening Post. 235:10+. D. 8, '62. Speaking out; Uncle Sam's rejects. George Walton.

Saturday Evening Post. 236:70. F. 9, '63. Unemployment and the reading problem.

Saturday Review. 43:28-9. F. 13, '60. Life devoted to world literacy. S. I. Hayakawa.

Saturday Review. 44:24. My. 27, '61. Vital statistics, 1961. R. L. Tobin.

Saturday Review. 46:75-7+. F. 16, '63. Life is fun in a smiling, fair-skinned world. Otto Klineberg.

School and Society. 81:145-9. My. 14, '55. Social class structure and the world educational situation. G. N. Brown.

School and Society. 89:207-8. Ap. 22, '61. First university literacy center; Baylor University, Waco, Texas. R. W. Cortright.

*School and Society. 89:371-2. N. 4, '61. World literacy and education. Gertrude Hildreth.

School and Society. 90:155-6. Ap. 7, '62. Abolition of illiteracy.

School and Society. 90:369+. N. 3, '62. UNESCO plan to cut adult illiteracy.

School and Society. 92:94-5. Mr. 7, '64. African nations urge eradication of illiteracy.

School and Society. 92:95+. Mr. 7, '64. Dangers of adult illiteracy. Francis Keppel.

School and Society. 92:179. Ap. 18, '64. School dropout and adult education. W. W. Brickman.

School and Society. 92:200. My. 2, '64. Thousands of teachers needed in Africa.

School Arts. 63:32-4. My. '64. High school dumping grounds. Margaret Venable.

School Life. 33:131-3. Je. '51. Illiteracy and manpower mobilization. Ambrose Caliver.

School Life. 34:90-1. Mr. '52. Literacy and the national welfare. H. M. Kilgore.

School Life. 40:13-14. D. '57. For a more literate nation. Ambrose Caliver.

School Life. 45:5-7+. F. '63. President's message on education, January 29, 1963. J. F. Kennedy.

*School Life. 45:5-7. Ap. '63. Culturally deprived child: a new view. Frank Riessman.

School Life. 45:18. Ap. '63. Illiteracy in the U.S. W. V. Grant.

Science News Letter. 77:326. My. 21, '60. Underprivileged teens.

Science News Letter. 83:150. Mr. 9, '63. World fifty per cent illiterate.

Science News Letter. 84:210. O. 5, '63. Homes affect mentality.

Senior Scholastic. 74:10-11. Ap. 10, '59. Missionary of A-B-C's.

Senior Scholastic. 83:44. O. 4, '63. How many of the world's people can read and write.

Senior Scholastic. 84:1T. Ap. 17, '64. Education and change.

Senior Scholastic. 84:1T-2T+. Ap. 24, '64. Scholastic teacher interviews: Francis Keppel.

Senior Scholastic. 84:5T-6T. Ap. 24, '64. Culturally deprived in the great cities. Frederick Bertolaet.

*Senior Scholastic. 84:13T-14T. Ap. 24, '64. Teachers and parents work together in depressed neighborhoods. G. C. Fusco.

Time. 75:50. Ja. 11, '60. Mass assault.

Time. 76:53-4+. N. 21, '60. Wasted talent.

Time. 80:48. D. 14, '62. Rx for infectious ignorance; R. W. Hilliard's program in Chicago.

UNESCO Chronicle. 10:9-12. Ja. '64. Decisive step for a world campaign against illiteracy.

*UNESCO Courier. 14:32-5. Je. '61. 70 million illiterates. Oscar Vera.

U.S. News & World Report. 55:8. Jl. 22, '63. Crime and illiteracy in the nation's capital.

United Nations Review. 10:34-5. D. '63. Eradication of illiteracy; excerpts from statement, October 18, 1963. René Maheu.

United Nations Review. 11:31-4. Ja. '64. Campaign for world literacy; Campaign against hunger and disease; Science and technology for development.

United Nations World. 5:25-7+. D. '51. Half the world is illiterate. C. L. Heymann.

Vital Speeches of the Day. 25:583-8. Jl. 15, '59. Each one teach one; address, April 3, 1959. F. C. Laubach.

Vital Speeches of the Day. 27:554-60. Jl. 1, '61. Social dynamite in our large cities; address, May 24, 1961. J. B. Conant.

Vital Speeches of the Day. 28:106-9. D. 1, '61. Tyranny of ignorance; address, September 29, 1961. N. P. Auburn.

*Wilson Library Bulletin. 38:345-8. D. '63. New books for the slum child. P. J. Groff.

Wilson Library Bulletin. 38:840-2+. Je. '64. Books as weapons.

*Wilson Library Bulletin. 38:844-51+. Je. '64. Federal aid for the illiterate. R. B. Minnis.
  Text of address delivered April 8, 1964, at conference on functional illiterates sponsored by American Book Publishers Council and American Textbook Publishers Institute.

Wisconsin Journal of Education. 89:19. Mr. '57. Literacy has new meanings. G. C. Boardman.